# LIFE/CHOICE

## The Theory of Just Abortion

### LLOYD STEFFEN

THE PILGRIM PRESS
Cleveland, Ohio

The Pilgrim Press, Cleveland, Ohio 44115

© 1994 by Lloyd Steffen

All rights reserved. Published 1994

Printed in the United States of America

The paper used in this publication is acid free

99 98 97 96 95 94 5 4 3 2 1

Library of Congress Cataloging-in-Publication Data

Steffen, Lloyd H., 1951–
Life/choice : the theory of just abortion / Lloyd Steffen.
p.   cm.
Includes bibliographical references and index.
ISBN 0-8298-0998-8
1. Abortion—Moral and ethical aspects.   I. Title.
HQ767.15.S74   1994
363.4'6—dc20
94-813
CIP

*For Em*

# Contents

# Preface

---

I have always liked the idea that a preface is a place for an author to show a kindness or two, and to acknowledge kindnesses that have helped bring a labor of writing to its conclusion. Before I acknowledge kindnesses I have received in the course of writing this book, I want to perform a service—a kind service, I hope—for the reader.

A person picking up a book on abortion may think that the world doesn't really need one more such book. The author of this particular book is a white male, which some readers might consider a disqualifying credential. And the title of the book ought to alert the reader that a healthy skepticism is in order. For if the author wants to argue for a morally moderate position on abortion, meaning that he thinks there is some way to bring pro-life and pro-choice positions together, one might suspect that he either does not understand the abortion issue in the slightest or, thinking he does, is in the grip of profound self-deception. If the reader has considered this and decides to look into the book despite these substantive reasons for not doing so, then I confess to being humbled in the face of such faith and open-mindedness and acknowledge that I owe that reader some token of appreciation.

The token I offer is this: a summary of the argument. I argue in this book that there is a morally moderate position on the abortion issue, which can mean only one thing: some abortions are morally permissible and others are not. The question, then, is to establish some basis for deciding which are which.

The "just abortion" theory presented here, which I ground in goods of life and values that persons on both sides of the abortion issue can affirm, states that persons in moral community, which includes all persons of good will, accept a moral presumption against abortion. I try to explain this in terms that I believe any non-absolutist on the abortion issue could affirm. I then argue that that moral presumption ordinarily holds with regard to pregnancy, the biological process whereby human beings promote the good of human life. The moral presumption serves to protect and promote the good of life ingredient in pregnancy.

The moral presumption at issue is only a presumption, however, and, accordingly, it does not express an absolute value about life or choice. It is in relation to the moral presumption against abortion that I then proceed to argue that the presumption can be lifted in the case of an unwanted pregnancy if certain conditions are met.

The six conditions I present as necessary for a just abortion are these: (1) that the evaluation that a pregnancy is unwanted be determined by competent authority; (2) that the abortion be based on a just cause, which involves evaluating individual and corporate (social) responsibility for unwanted pregnancy; (3) that the abortion be a last resort, which requires that adoption be considered but that it not be pre-judged as always preferable to abortion, morally speaking, since adoption presents moral problems of its own; (4) that the abortion not pose a greater medical risk to the pregnant woman than continued pregnancy; (5) that by proceeding with the abortion, one is not subverting the value of life, but rather is acting to suspend the moral presumption against abortion only to reinstate that presumption and thus continue to honor the good of life ingredient in pregnancy; and (6) that a moral rather than a biologically or developmentally based criterion set a limit for the period of time when an abortion can be justifiably performed, that criterion being the promise made by the pregnant woman, either explicitly or implicitly, to bring the fetus to term.

These six criteria, set in relation to a moral presumption against abortion, define the formal elements of the just abortion theory advanced here.

I say many other things in these pages—that abortion should be accepted as identifying a killing; that the social policy debate over abortion has obscured the moral debate; that a moderate moral position must assume a pro-choice social policy, although putting restrictions on abortion, within certain limits, is appropriate; and that the constitutional debate over abortion is properly a debate over freedom of religion. In all that I say, I put forth the idea that abortion is morally complex and problematic, and that those who present it as otherwise are distorting its moral meaning. Such distortion is commonplace in the public policy debate over abortion, in my opinion; I argue in this essay against continuing the abortion debate as if the moral meaning of abortion is clear, simple, and uncontroversial. Only those who affirm moral absolutes approach abortion this way, and I oppose moral absolutism. I could have subtitled this work "An Essay against Moral Absolutism," but I recalled an old friend, the late theologian Roger Hazelton, who was fond of saying, "People are more likely to be right in what they affirm than in what they deny." So rather than emphasizing what I am against—moral absolutism—I emphasize what I am for, namely, the conjoining of life and choice in a moderate perspective that seeks to construct moral meaning in a world that is imperfect. In that world, moral quandaries do arise and present us with real problems. Our capacity to address those problems is affected by our limited wisdom, our lack of compassion, and by the complexity of the world and of the human heart.

That summary statement is my kindness, my token of appreciation. The reader who picked this book up skeptically now has reason to continue—or not.

I have some words of appreciation to extend. I am grateful to my students in ethics classes over the years who have provoked me into rethinking the abortion issue, and many other issues as well. I am grateful to colleagues and friends who have conversed with me on this issue and who have offered me support and criticism—and no aspersions should be directed at any of those whom I name here. Gratitude for help and friendship is certainly no reason to infer that those to whom it is directed agree with what I have written.

I especially appreciate the encouragement and support of Tom Kasulis, Tom Poole, John Thomas, Ian Birky, William Hamilton, and my colleagues in the Religion Studies department at Lehigh University. A special word of thanks must be given to Professor Michael Raposa at Lehigh, who read portions of the manuscript and whose humor and engaged criticism were a constant source of support. I acknowledge my indebtedness to Dr. Stan Yellin, director of the Lehigh University Health Center, for answering my medical questions and directing me to medical resources when I asked for help. I appreciate my friends and colleagues at Lafayette College, especially Dr. Gary Miller, who arranged for me to speak at Lafayette on the topic "Is a Moderate Moral Position on Abortion Possible?," and Professor Stephen Lammers, who graciously read the entire manuscript and offered me challenging criticisms that made the final product better. Richard Brown at Pilgrim Press has provided me with advice and direction, and I thank him for all his good efforts in support of this project, and for the suggestions he directed my way as critic and intermediary for anonymous readers.

I am also grateful for having had the chance to present some of my thoughts about abortion at the 1989 Craigville Theological Colloquy and at a meeting of the Superior Wisconsin chapter of the National Organization for Women, and for an invitation to participate in a conversation/debate about abortion sponsored by the Wisconsin Right to Life Committee. For the invitations I received and the opportunities I was graciously granted to offer my perspectives, I am truly grateful.

My deepest word of thanks, however, goes to Emmajane Finney, whose support of me at some mysterious point extended to support of this project. For her criticisms, for her support, for her sensitive yet decisive reading of the manuscript, and for all that she has offered as together we have tried to perform balancing acts with schedules in the face of constant demands placed on us by Nathan, Sam, and Will, I say the "thank you" that is best said on the dedication page.

# Introduction

<hr>

## RECLAIMING ABORTION AS A MORAL PROBLEM

Abortion may be defined several ways. A *Clinical Manual of Gynecology* defines it as "the loss or termination of pregnancy prior to viability." What is lost or terminated, according to the manual, is an abortus less than 500 grams in weight and less than twenty weeks in gestational age.[1] The Committee on Terminology of the American College of Obstetrics and Gynecology has proposed the following as its definition of abortion: "Expulsion or extraction of all or part of the placenta or membranes, without an identifiable fetus, or with a liveborn infant or a stillborn infant weighing less than 500 gm. In the absence of known weight, an estimated length of gestation of less than 20 completed weeks (139 days) calculated from the first day of the last normal menstrual period may be used."[2]

The technical language of these definitions gives no hint that what is being referred to is perhaps the most inflammatory and divisive topic confronting society today. No footnotes appear to remind the reader about the fractious interpretive disputes surrounding abortion. No efforts are made to clarify that the sparse, clean language of "extraction," "gram weight," and "gestational age" is referring to an intended death of a developing form of human life. A medical definition may tell us what abortion refers to in a clinical, descriptive sense, but it does not tell us what abortion means. Judgments are withheld. Evaluations of the medical facts are not offered.

The morally neutral language of a dispassionate medical textbook definition of abortion is misleading. Such language fosters the illusion that somewhere a level of interpretation exists at which abortion presents itself as a medical event that is no more value-laden than other medical extractions with which we are familiar, such as pulling a tooth, removing an infected appendix, or excising a tumor. But abortion is anything but value-free. And referring to these other, less controversial extractions for purposes of comparison does not provide a value-free model, since they are presumably good, life-enhancing procedures that promote human well-being. If pulling a tooth is not value-free, aborting a developing form of human life—whether as conceptus, embryo, or fetus—cannot be value-free.

Abortion has fractured a nation, threatened the rule of law, disrupted religious communities, divided families, decided elections, spurred violence, and presented women—and couples—facing unwanted pregnancies with difficult personal decisions. No medical definition could explore these ramifications, much less explain them through the descriptive resources of gram weight and gestational age. But these ramifications are central to understanding abortion, and by mentioning them we remind ourselves that abortion is a topic of interpretive conflict. What is in dispute is not medical meaning, but moral meaning. All the controversy that rages in the abortion debate over life and death, goodness and wrongdoing, values, rights, personhood, and even social policy derives from a fundamental division that has emerged in contemporary American society. Disagreement over moral meaning has created a social debate the likes of which has rarely been witnessed in this country's life.

The most strident voices heard today in this debate belong to those who have seemingly resolved the moral perplexities surrounding abortion. Although many people are not certain about the moral meaning of abortion, most people have decided the public policy question and endorse the goal of either prohibiting abortions or, to one degree or another, allowing them.

As the public policy debate has polarized, the uncertainties and ambiguities that ordinarily would be at play in a moral debate over so complex an issue have faded from view. In our current cultural climate, where moral beliefs have hardened to justify public policy positions, it is doubtful whether people any longer approach abortion primarily as a moral problem. The extreme, all-or-nothing social policy goal of prohibiting abortions, which is the center of the political controversy, has so radicalized the terms of the debate that it is common to hear advocates on both sides of the question grounding their social policy positions in moral beliefs that are extreme, absolutist, and free from messy moral problems. A social policy debate that forces people to decide for or against the extreme option of prohibition invites moral arguments that are as extreme and all-or-nothing as the social policy alternatives themselves. Moral conversation has become a debate between moral absolutes, each side convinced that its social policy position rests on certainty about the moral meaning of abortion.[3] And people who are certain about the moral meaning of abortion often do not confront abortion as a moral problem.

I contend that abortion *is* a moral problem and that the moral meaning of abortion is not so clear as the public policy debate indicates. Furthermore, I believe that many people are still troubled by abortion to the point that if given the opportunity to reflect on moral meaning, they would opt for a more complex response than that which issues from a yes-or-no vote on the question of prohibition. Many people still understand abortion to be a moral problem at some basic level not addressed in the public policy debate, and many who have made their decisions about the social policy question on abortion are left with some uncertainty and still wonder why their discomfort with abortion has not been articulated in the debate itself. There lurks a suspicion in the minds of many that abortion is a morally complex issue that cannot be reduced to the same kind of either/or option that is at stake in the social policy debate. Many people recognize that value commitments, metaphysical views of the person, and religious beliefs are the true source of controversy over abortion, and their frustration with the debate stems from a recognition that these conflicts have been obscured and distorted by the political debate.

In the pages that follow, I give voice to the perspective that says abortion is and always will be a moral problem, and that opting for one public policy solution over the other is not a productive way to decipher that problem or even adequately address it. To hold that abortion is a moral problem requires that one avoid the temptations to simplify that have emerged in the public policy debate and refuse absolutist solutions.

The case that abortion is still a moral problem can be made by looking at the extreme views on abortion and seeking the moral truth that has been radicalized in each. The challenge, then, is to stand between both truths as truths and to touch both at once. Accomplishing that will not only restore abortion to its neglected status as a moral problem, but will, more importantly, restore a sense of moral complexity to our deliberations about the issue, even in our public policy debate. My purpose here is to restore that sense of moral complexity, then suggest a structure and guide for those deliberations, which I am terming a theory of just abortion.

As members of a moral community that is divided against itself over the abortion issue, we have not found a reasonable way, or even a reasonable theory, that allows us to see the common underlying value commitments that persons in the moral community—even those with differing views about abortion—necessarily share. On the abortion issue, we have obscured the truth that a moral presumption against abortion is held even by persons who are, in social policy terms, pro-choice. And we have failed to point out to those who oppose the pro-choice policy that when they acknowledge certain circumstances so serious that an abortion could justifiably be considered, they are no longer the absolutist pro-life purists they think they are.

The just abortion theory seeks to identify the truth at the core of opposing absolutist positions, then bring them together. Just abortion steers clear of extremism and absolutism in favor of a morally moderate position; and moral moderation on the abortion issue means one thing: that some abortions are morally justifiable and others are not. The problem one faces—and now we are confronted with a true moral problem for which absolutist responses are irrelevant and inappropriate—is how to distinguish those abortions that are morally justifiable from those that are not. The moral status of any particular abortion, then, is an open question requiring analysis and evaluation. And this is what actually confronts people who, because of life circumstance and situation, consider abortion. They confront a problem about what to do and how to decide.

The theory of just abortion as I present it will not only defend the social policy of choice—it will assume it. If at least some abortions are permissible, then people who face decisions about abortion must have room in the social and political environment for making those decisions. A morally moderate position on abortion will require that the law not deprive persons of their responsibility to make difficult decisions in the light of the many variables that come into play in individual cases. It will require that the law not intervene to prevent these variables from being considered, out of hand, as irrelevant. Only a morally absolutist view could summarily dismiss all the variables that would affect decisions in individual cases. As a non-absolutist theory, just abortion will require that the social policy context of choice be preserved as the logical extension of just abortion thinking. Put another way, just abortion theory affirms pro-choice as the social policy option that appropriately accompanies a morally moderate position.

Just abortion will accept, on the pro-life side, that members of a moral community hold a moral presumption against abortion. Underlying this presumption is a moral commitment to the view that life is good and that pregnancy, the biological process required for the continuation of life, is, in the first instance, a good to be protected and promoted. In a perfect world, pregnancy and the good of life being promoted by pregnancy would be affirmed in every situation without qualification. The desirability of every pregnancy could be affirmed. Every pregnancy would be wanted.

Just abortion, however, acknowledges that ours is an imperfect world. It recognizes that not every pregnancy is wanted, and, more important, it does not absolutize the moral presumption against abortion. Just abortion will attend to the situations and circumstances of real persons as they confront a decision about how to evaluate the good of life involved in pregnancy in relation to other goods that are also important. What just abortion provides is a moral framework for advancing the non-absolutist view that situations may arise that would allow us to justify abortion in various circumstances if certain conditions—the six criteria I spelled out earlier—are met.

As I have already indicated, America's abortion debate has been reduced to terms that distort the moral complexity of the issue. As a practical matter, abortion has actually become morally unproblematic for many people, and I have suggested that the public policy debate has effected a hardening of attitudes while encouraging people to express moral certainty, even absolutism, as they defend their public policy positions. In advocating a just abortion perspective, I am assuming that abortion does not reduce so easily to the terms in which we have often framed the debate. My specific thesis is that we acknowledge both the moral presumption against abortion and the possibility that if certain specific moral requirements are met an abortion can be morally justified.

Beyond that, I shall invite readers to reflect on the role that societies play in promoting abortion as a response to unwanted pregnancy. I shall raise, for instance, the question of social and corporate responsibility. If we shift the focus of the abortion debate away from legal issues to moral issues, we have to confront the fact that not only is abortion not a good of life to be promoted, but a high number of abortions in society is the result of conditions that allow such high numbers to develop and persist. How are we as a society confronting our social responsibility for a situation reasonable persons would like to see reversed? Too often, we simply turn away from such serious moral questions and redirect our attention to an individual woman facing a sometimes lonely and always difficult personal decision.

Here we make a terrible mistake in our moral analyses of abortion. For it is clearly relevant to our analysis that poverty exists in our country, that racism and sexism are common, that some women are denied the kinds of educational opportunity and financial means necessary if they are to act consistently with their own desires to avoid unwanted pregnancies. The social complicity issue forces us to consider the possibility that many of those who, because of poverty and disadvantage, are least able to elect abortion when confronted with an unwanted pregnancy are actually the persons in the strongest moral position for justifying one. It also reminds us that the abortion debate has been dominated by relatively affluent white Americans able to organize and operate effectively in the political system. We must consider once again the role that poverty and racism play as relevant factors in our analysis of moral meaning. If our society has created an abortion-approving ethos, as pro-life critics often charge, then we must think about what we do collectively, as a society, to contribute to the problem of unwanted pregnancies among persons who are least able to prevent them. Placing a moral burden on disempowered persons without taking account of all that a society contributes to their disempowerment, which is certainly a relevant factor in assessing an individual's ability to exercise control over her reproductive life, is the equivalent of putting on moral blinders and blaming the victim. Societies actively participate in the creation of conditions that inevitably give rise to increasing numbers of unwanted pregnancies and abortions. Just abortion will take social, corporate responsibility into account in its determination of just cause.

I am seeking to articulate what I believe is the sound moral intuition of many people on the abortion issue: that abortions should be avoided and certainly not promoted, but that there are occasions when electing abortion as a response to unwanted pregnancy is both responsible and morally justified. This intuition grows out of an understanding that in an imperfect world, abortion will sometimes not only be a permissible thing to do, but the right thing, even the best thing, to do.

## A PERSONAL NOTE

Although this book is the product of more than a decade of teaching and learning about abortion in the ethics classroom, the particular impetus for this work came from some reactions I received after speaking about the issue at a 1989 theological colloquy.[4] I had not thought about categorizing my position until I heard myself introduced as one who seemed to be offering a moderate position on abortion. After hearing two other speakers offer articulate viewpoints for their more readily identifiable pro-life and pro-choice positions, I began to see that my argument didn't neatly conform to either.

I received some interesting questions and responses after making my appearance at the podium. From some of the criticisms, I could not tell if I had helped clarify things or simply made the issue even more confusing. Before I left, however, a church pastor came up to me and said, "I have been so confused over the abortion issue for so long. You didn't give me any definite answers—but you honored my questions and my doubts, and helped me to see that being uncertain and even bewildered by this issue is actually an authentic place to stand."

Because I did not speak out on the abortion issue to offer easy answers or absolutist solutions, but to clarify the moral issues for purposes of moral and theological reflection, that reaction, while it may not have been typical, was gratifying to hear. For moral and theological reflection does not reduce abortion to simple terms, as if it were a problem in mathematics. Rather, reflection brings to bear information and moral concerns that make abortion increasingly resistant to easy, all-or-nothing solutions.

In the days following that first public talk on the issue, I became convinced that the "no easy answer" perspective I was urging deserved more of a hearing. From reactions to subsequent talks I gave—one at a local National Organization for Women forum, the other a debate with the head of the Wisconsin Right to Life Committee—I began to think that a more developed picture of this morally moderate position was called for.

## JUST WAR THEORY AND JUST ABORTION

The moral questions behind my argument of this work are simple: Are there any conditions that, if met, would allow us to evaluate an abortion as morally permissible? Are there ever circumstances that might *require* an abortion as an appropriate moral response? If so, what are those conditions and circumstances? This way of asking questions about moral problems is familiar to students of ethics and moral philosophers. For me, the tradition that best embodies this approach to moral questions through conditional thinking is the one that has grown up around "just war."

I acknowledge that a theory of just abortion is problematic at the outset, not because its debt to just war theory is undeniable, but because just war theory is not, for many morally sensitive persons, particularly credible in the light of certain events in America's recent history. Just war theory was pressed into service by America's political leadership during the invasion of Panama (Operation Just Cause) and in the 1991 Persian Gulf War. Just war theory was employed by governmental authorities in self-serving, tendentious, and misleading ways almost, but not quite, deserving to be discredited by the way those public employments were performed.[5]

That just war theory could be so seriously distorted in the midst of armed conflict was made possible, in part, by the fact that it is not well understood.[6] For instance, America's political leadership during the Gulf War carefully abbreviated the conditions under which use of force may be morally legitimated. There was no public discussion by high governmental authorities that just war theory was built upon a clear and abiding presumption against the use of force—that is, that it was designed to promote alternatives to violence and encourage the restraint of force. Given that the theory was so easily adapted to serve a foreign policy objective and manipulated to justify a use of force already decided upon for political and economic reasons, just war looks all too suspect as a philosophical model.

Experience with this model as it has been used can and should provoke skepticism and call forth reservations. But I hold that just war is of value as a framework of moral analysis that offers a non-absolutist way of protecting a moral presumption for peace and non-violence. It identifies a common discourse for moral conversation and invites discussion among persons from a variety of perspectives. It sets the perimeter for moral debate by establishing moral concerns and conditions within a field of widely acceptable moral discourse; it establishes a framework for moral interpretation and analysis that allows for meaningful debate and conversation about a proposed use of force; it articulates moral markers that are of common interest to persons on both sides of a particular policy debate and to which both sides can appeal through a common moral discourse. (Objections to the use of force by President Bush's own military advisers appealed to the just war criterion of last resort, because some advisers questioned whether Operation Desert Storm ought to proceed if economic sanctions had not been given adequate time to work.) The conditions for lifting the presumption against the use of force are stringent and difficult to meet, but the theory insists that they be met. In an imperfect world, where force sometimes presents itself as an option of last resort, meeting such moral requirements is the only way to ensure that the demands of justice are met while seeking to preserve the moral presumption against the use of force.

The structure, rather than the details, of just war theory can be successfully replicated and applied to other moral issues and problems. Although I shall not simply transfer and correlate just war specifics to the question of abortion, I shall endorse the just war framework as a relevant model for non-absolutist thinking about abortion. A theory of just abortion will serve two important functions. First, in a common moral discourse, it will identify and seek to preserve a moral presumption that life is itself a good of life. Specifically, it will recognize that a developing human being possesses this good of life and that this good ought to be promoted and deserves to be protected. The theory will accept that this moral presumption will hold in most cases of pregnancy. Yet, because a just abortion theory is non-absolutist both theoretically and practically, it will also recognize human limitations and fallibility. This leads to the second function of the theory, which is that it provides, in a common moral discourse, a framework for evaluating the moral meaning of abortion in individual situations and circumstances. Putting the theory to work in specific situations will assist persons as they seek to make responsible choices—that is, choices that have been tested according to certain morally relevant concerns and criteria. Just abortion theory will specify the conditions under which the moral presumption at the heart of the theory can justifiably be lifted.

In the pages that follow, I shall try to open up a conversation with the reader about abortion as a moral problem. I have tried to focus the discussion in such a way as to invite moral reflection back into a broader, public discourse. Accordingly, I have sought to address people, and especially people in the church, who are dissatisfied with the various options that have been offered by church declarations and public policy directives and by other groups whose ideological commitments are expressed in an all-or-nothing rhetoric of certainty about the moral meaning of abortion—a certainty that is hardly merited.

This book represents my understanding of what a moderate position on abortion will have to look like. I shall argue that abortion is a troubling issue, that it should be troubling, and that those who render it in some way non-troubling distort the issue morally. Pro-choice advocates will find that I challenge some of the often flaunted justifications for allowing choice. Pro-life advocates will find that I undermine some of their cherished justifications, and they will undoubtedly argue that mine is simply one more pro-choice position. That is not so. I offer here not a public policy statement, but a moral position on an issue that requires a particular public policy (freedom of choice) so that it can be addressed as if it were primarily a moral, as distinct from a legal or social policy, issue. I neither avoid nor disconnect from the public policy debate but simply argue for framing the debate in such a way that public policy solutions can be seen as premature or even unwarranted, given the moral uncertainty that surrounds various cases, kinds of cases, and broader social issues that impinge on the question of corporate responsibility.

Those uncertain about abortion, those somewhat frightened by the absolutism that has emerged from pronouncements expressing a variety of ideological stances on abortion, will, I hope, find this an argument of practical significance. I offer it hoping it will allow for informed and justifiable action based not only on factual information and values of undeniable goodness, but also on uncertainty and doubt, which is to say, in theological terms, "in fear and trembling."

# 1

# The Good of Life

An abortion is successfully performed when pregnancy is terminated and a developing form of human life—the conceptus, the embryo, the fetus—dies. Its death is foreseen and intended. It dies because someone kills it. Abortion, therefore, refers to a killing.

⟨The moral meaning of the killing that occurs in abortion is in dispute, as is the moral status of the abortus itself.⟩What is not in dispute is the fact that human beings in moral community value human life and consider it to be a basic good that should be promoted and protected. Killing deprives persons of this basic good. The moral community thus regards killing as a transgression or moral violation of the most serious kind and does not sanction or justify killing except for specific and morally compelling reasons.

For all the moral questions that the topic provokes, abortion is a common solution to the problem of unwanted pregnancy in the United States, as in many other countries. It is estimated that on any given day more than 150,000 abortions are performed in the world—or 55 million a year. The United States contributes an estimated 1.5 million abortions to that yearly total.[1] Moral reflection must seek to understand what it means

that abortions are not uncommon, that there may be as many as
two abortions for every three live births worldwide. One interpretation worth considering is the following. The high number
of abortions suggests that the procedure is widely available in a
variety of social, political, and cultural settings; availability suggests widespread legal, medical, and social sanction of abortion;
and societal sanction itself suggests that where abortions are
common, they are considered to be something other than a clear
and obvious evil to be avoided at all costs.

The fact that abortion entails a killing but that it has clearly
escaped general condemnation as a moral evil does not allow us
to draw any hard conclusions about the moral meaning of abortion. For it is also the case that abortion is seldom discussed as if
it were a positive and desirable good that could be recommended
or encouraged.(Not even those who support the right to choose
abortion hold it to be a positive good, for abortion rights advocates have lent strong support to programs and policies aimed at
increasing access to affordable birth control, the effect of which
would be to reduce the number of abortions.)

So abortion is not, as the high number of abortions in the
world today indicates, an obvious evil that is typically avoided or
universally condemned. Yet neither is it a desired good. If even
supporters of the right to choose abortion want to see the number
of abortions reduced; if even they are motivated by the good they
see in reducing that number and idealize an end to the need for
abortion—"Every child a wanted child," as the Planned Parenthood slogan goes—then abortion is clearly not regarded any-
where as a positive good.

(Some people regard abortion as a monstrous and avoidable
evil. For others it is a difficult but necessary option that makes it
possible for people to seek in good faith a humane solution to the
problem of unwanted pregnancy.) Still others find abortion so
bewildering and mysterious a problem that knowing how to evaluate its moral status seems beyond the measure of human ability.
Yet, for all this evaluative disagreement and confusion, no rational voice heard in America's contemporary abortion debate is
seriously proposing that abortion be evaluated as an intrinsically
desirable good that all of us ought to promote. This identifies the

point at which I want to begin to consider the moral meaning of abortion.

It is from this point that we shall work toward a theory of just abortion. We must begin a moral evaluation of abortion not with an analysis of *Roe v. Wade*; not with the murder of a doctor known to perform abortions by an anti-abortionist; and not with anecdotes from physicians whose opposition to abortions began, as did physician-essayist Richard Selzer's, with disgust at seeing bags of aborted fetuses spilled out of garbage trucks on a street behind a hospital.[2] We must begin our investigation by thinking about what is good and what killing means in relation to goodness. For abortion involves a killing, and no investigation into the moral meaning of abortion can refuse to acknowledge this descriptive fact.

We must remind ourselves, however, that not all killings are morally controversial. Despite the fact that moral communities universally honor life as a good and seek to promote and protect that good, they have not prohibited killing so much as they have restricted it.[3] Some killings are part of everyday life—the weeds pulled from the garden; the cockroach poisoned behind the water pipes; the bacteria that perish when we use a mouthwash, or a deodorant, or a foot powder. Some killings are laudable since they actually promote life. Examples would include the cell death that occurs when surgeons excise a tumor, or the elimination of animal or insect pests that could irreparably damage a necessary human food supply. What moral codes prohibit is the unjustified killing of members of the moral community. In thinking about killing we must recognize that killings, even those that involve members of the moral community, do not all mean the same thing. Some are more serious than others. Even animal rights advocates who might argue that a steer ought to be included in the moral community would concede that the intentional killing of a human person is a more serious matter, morally speaking, than the killing of a steer. Some killings that involve members of the moral community are generally regarded as justifiable, as when one incidentally kills an aggressor in the course of defending oneself. And some killings that involve human beings will always present themselves as morally problematic.

The killing that occurs in various acts of warfare, in state-sponsored executions, and in(abortion are clearly in the category of questionable, at least in the sense that the moral community continues to debate whether, or under what conditions, such killing can be morally justified.)

Consideration of this issue will lead us to articulate a theory of just abortion. My present task, however, is to clarify the meaning and value of the goods that are challenged by the killing that occurs in abortion. It is in this issue that just abortion—and the moral life itself—is grounded.

## THE VALUE OF LIFE

Because life is universally regarded as a basic good of life, the act of extinguishing a life requires moral reflection. Basic goods, which are those that are necessary to human well-being, are so highly valued in our life in moral community that we not only promote them but protect them from violation.(Killing violates the good of life) Moral communities, through moral codes and social systems, have sought to engender respect for this good, honoring its increase, as the Hebrews did in recording God's first commandment as a charge to be fruitful and multiply, while also proscribing various acts that would diminish life, lessen respect for it, or actually extinguish it. But why is life, which is a biological process, so highly valued? And is it the highest value, even an absolute value?

To say, as we do in the moral traditions of the west, that life is one of the goods of life may not seem to be saying much. Goods of life is an uninviting expression, but it is not mysterious. The very simplicity and utter commonness of the language evokes a deeper moral meaning, which is accessible to us all. In a practical sense, all that is being referred to in the expression goods of life are those essentials of well-being that are necessary if human beings are to flourish.

We can discern the basic goods of life by identifying what is most important to people, what it is they value most highly, what they regard as essential for life that seems meaningful, purposeful, and significant.[4] Asking people what is most important to them would elicit many particulars, and there would be some variation in response from person to person and shifts in emphasis from culture to culture. But despite that variation, all adequate listings of the goods of life would include certain general categories. My specific list would include the following:

- life itself;
- physical integrity, self-consciousness, and the capacity for interacting meaningfully in one's environment;
- the capacity to experience pleasure and aesthetic enjoyment;
- the freedom and ability to work, play, and pursue speculative knowledge;
- the capacity to form loving relationships with other persons (friendships) and with a transcendent Other (religion);
- the development of a personal identity that reflects character and the cohesiveness of personal integrity;
- practical reasonableness, which is the good of life that connects being and action and grounds all moral reflection.[5]

The goods of life ground a moral ontology of the human. They identify features of human being that are intrinsically valuable; that is, they do not derive value from some good that could be considered even more basic. And they express goodness itself, conveying a vision of goodness in the concrete values where goodness, which is hard to define, is recognizable; for even if we cannot always say what the good is, we usually know it when we see it.[6]

I want to consider goodness and its expression in the various goods of life as a particular way of gaining access to moral meaning, which is the problem at issue in the abortion question. Abortion is a problem in moral relations, and some notion of goodness is at stake when the moral meaning of the pregnant woman's relation to the developing form of human life she carries is uncertain or in dispute. It is goodness that is at issue when thinking about pregnancy, unwanted pregnancy, and a woman's exercise of moral autonomy in community; it is goodness that, as we shall see momentarily, checks the tendency of human beings to create moral absolutes then ground them in illusions of objective certainty about moral meaning.

Attending to goodness provides one avenue of approach to thinking about moral complexity and the difficulty well-meaning persons have when trying to make good and responsible decisions about how to act. Goodness moves us, motivates us to act, incites us to attend to our interactions with others.[7] Without goodness, without the specific goods of life in which goodness manifests itself, persons would not be moved to seek happiness or fulfillment or to fashion for themselves a meaningful life with others. The vision of goodness that is embodied in the concrete goods of life grounds the moral life and establishes the foundations for moral community. The goods of life present themselves not as options for lifestyle choices, but as necessities that all individuals require if they are to live well and flourish.

## LIFE: A RELATIONAL VALUE

We recognize life, the essential datum or ground of all biological reality, to be a necessary and intrinsic good, the most fundamental condition of human well-being. But that recognition does not necessarily imply that the good of life can be isolated from other goods, or that the value of life will always override other values and dictate how one assesses questions about moral meaning when life itself may be in question.

The good of life itself holds a preeminent place in our thinking about goods, for life is the only good that cannot be reacquired if it is taken away or lost.[8] And it is preeminent in the sense that it is prerequisite to our acquiring other goods—one must possess life before one can enjoy the goods of consciousness or develop a capacity for aesthetic enjoyment, or work, or speculative knowledge. Life is an intrinsic good in the sense that its value is not derived from some more basic good.

But acknowledging the good of life as preeminent and basic does not mean that life should therefore be regarded as an absolute good, one that must always and under every circumstance supersede other values. Values, and the goods of life themselves, lack meaning outside of the relational matrix where human beings encounter and receive them. By holding that the good of life has a special, preeminent place in a hierarchy of values, it does not follow that life is a value unrelated to other values or that it is always the highest value in the sense that it must be preserved at all cost, even at the expense of other values. In the moral community, no value—however basic—has meaning independent of its relationship to other values.

The relevance of this relational view of values to the abortion issue can be discerned in particular arguments in the abortion debate. For instance, the argument is sometimes made that the developing form of human life, even at the conceptus or embryo stage, is deserving of absolute protection. The reason it deserves protection, the argument goes, is not because it is capable of enjoying the other goods of life, but because it deserves to be included in the moral community on the basis of possessing the basic and preeminent good of life itself. The good of life is so honored that possession of this good is deemed sufficient to withstand the challenge of any other goods of life that might be involved in a particular pregnancy. Establishing that life is present, even at the moment an ovum is fertilized, suffices to warrant the protection of the good of life—at all costs.

This argument does more than accept the good of life as a preeminent value—it makes life itself an absolute value. This position, practically speaking, amounts to saying that the presence of the good of life is itself sufficient for establishing objective certainty about moral meaning. Other goods, whether singly or in combination, ought not to affect our assessment of the good of life or our obligation to protect it from harm. We would not, in this view, need to concern ourselves with the mother's well-being when a pregnancy endangers her life or psychological integrity. Neither would we need to consider what follows morally when a human embryo is known to be severely deformed genetically and when the individual who would develop from it would have no reasonable prospect of flourishing as a competent human being able to enjoy, even in a minimal way, the other goods of life.

Absolute values spring from a very human desire to acquire true knowledge and certainty about moral meaning, and they are attractive because they allow us to avoid the messy business of constructing moral meaning on the basis of necessarily incomplete knowledge, the ambiguity of value relationships, and an inescapable logical fuzziness that is present in every act of interpretation. Reason, emotion, experience, and all that goes into developing humane and sympathetic human relationships conspire to resist this attraction, however. The good of practical reasonableness opposes the efforts some of us make to attach to any particular value or good of life the weighty modifier "absolute," for doing so disrelates that good from all others and leads to inevitable moral contradiction. Fortunately, value absolutes are usually short-lived when they pop up in serious moral discussions, but we must remember that they do arise and that they exert a dangerous influence.

To affirm some good of life as an absolute value allows one to claim certainty about moral meaning. In the abortion issue, if one says that a fetus is innocent human life, and innocent human life is construed to be an absolute good deserving of absolute protection, then the moral meaning of abortion is absolutely clear. Similarly, were one to say hypothetically [9] that a woman's right to decide about continuing a pregnancy is an expression of autonomy that cannot be affected or restricted in any way by others, then the moral meaning of proposed restrictions on abortion is also absolutely clear. The desire for moral certainty can come to be so highly valued that it invests particular goods with the power to subordinate other goods of life to it. When this happens, the result is the inflexible moral and intellectual postures we associate with fanaticism.

Fanaticism is a form of moral irrationality that denies the good of practical reasonableness and disengages the good of speculative knowledge. Fanatics do not permit the questioning or qualification of values. Rather, they interpret certain values as absolute norms, then hold to those norms no matter what. A fanatic is one who, in the name of an absolute value, would sacrifice the basic goods of life to that value, even sacrificing the absolute value itself.

Value absolutism in the abortion debate will always be a destructive force, for it authorizes the absolutist to disregard other goods to which the good of life is related and turn away the appeals of practical reasonableness. Pro-life fanatics who resort to violence and endanger pregnant women suffer the peculiar fate of all value absolutists: they contradict themselves and may even end up destroying the very lives (the "unborn children") they are seeking at all cost to preserve.

A morally moderate approach to abortion must begin by affirming that if no one good of life is absolute, then the goods of life and the values that attach to them are interrelated. A project to construct such an approach must challenge, and finally oppose, moral positions that express a moral certainty derived from absolute values. A morally moderate approach will then concern itself with the task of keeping the various goods of life in play so that they affect and balance each other. Affirming a relational view of values allows us to see how a picture of moderate moral meaning begins to develop, one that requires persons to honor the good of life, although not in a way that disrelates it from all other goods.

## FROM GOODS TO MORAL PROBLEMS

Eliminating moral absolutes makes possible moral problems. If abortion is to be considered a moral problem, it has to be established that abortion involves a conflict between values. The abortion debate has generally proceeded by determining that rights are in conflict. Rights, to clarify the term, are claims that embody fundamental values. As the abortion debate has polarized, the value conflict that has emerged pits a pregnant woman's right to make choices about her reproductive life against a fetus' right to continued existence.

But behind this simple construal of the value conflict are important questions concerning a mother's autonomy; the moral status of the fetus—whether it is a member of the moral community; and the role of society in helping to resolve these fundamental questions of value. These are issues that any book on abortion must address. But these issues assume value conflicts, which moral absolutists eliminate. If abortion is to qualify as a moral problem, it must be so construed that it confronts people with a genuine conflict involving deeply held values. The conflict must be of such a character that it is not easily resolved, and for a variety of reasons, including the following:

- all the relevant facts are not known;
- uncertainty, even confusion, surrounds the facts one does have, which can lead to different and arguable descriptions of what is being subjected to analysis;
- disputes arise over the values or moral perspectives appealed to, calling into question not the worthiness of the values appealed to, but their relevance to the issue at hand;
- the metaphysical, moral, and religious assumptions that support the values one does hold can be so employed as to yield objective certainty about moral meaning, which is to misunderstand fundamentally moral meaning as the constructed product of interpretation.

The conflict in values that lies at the heart of every moral problem may even expose conflicts that resist any kind of solution. When this point is reached, we face an actual moral dilemma. Moral dilemmas are those conflicts in which we face the unwelcome prospect that we will commit a moral transgression and offend against our preference to act morally whatever course of action we choose.[10]

When we confront moral problems, we typically respond by tentatively proposing courses of action and opening ourselves to legitimate questions about moral meaning that challenge our perspectives and engage us in reflective response. Abortion is not addressed primarily as a moral problem. If it were, the debate would be proceeding in a fundamentally different way than it is today. Participants on both sides of the issue would attend to issues of individual and corporate responsibility. They would proceed on the assumption that individuals facing difficult personal decisions deserve to be treated with compassion. And the debate would not focus on difficult alternatives to abortion, like adoption, that are described simply and unfairly as morally non-problematic ways out of any value conflict over abortion. Those who advocate adoption as a morally non-problematic solution to unwanted pregnancy assume that a mother who brings her pregnancy to term and then gives her baby away does not confront an issue in moral relations where human well-being is at stake. This view is not only highly questionable, but it assumes that the value of life supersedes all others: it reflects value absolutism in another form.⟩

⟨Abortion will never lend itself to resolution by those who claim to have the only possible and absolutely certain resolution, for if such certainty were really available and such a resolution possible, the moral meaning of abortion would not be in dispute, and disputes that did arise would appear unintelligible and irrational.⟩

If abortion holds the status of a moral problem rather than a moral certainty, any position that claims to have access to all the objective facts relevant to assessing its moral meaning should be greeted with suspicion. Some persons base their decisions about abortion on the certainty science can provide. They hope to invoke what science knows about the biological status of the fetus to draw moral conclusions.

But appeals to science cannot determine what the moral status of the fetus is or ought to be. Science is not competent to answer this question, whatever science might tell us about the unique genetic make-up of individual fetuses, and whatever technological advances based on science might be introduced into the moral debate. Science can provide certain facts, many of which can be shown to be relevant to the interpretive question of moral evaluation. But relevance must be established, and what any particular facts mean for purposes of moral evaluation is strictly speaking a question of ethics and not a question of science, even if individual scientists wish to comment on those facts and offer their moral interpretations. A biologist who speaks to the abortion issue as a biologist and as a moral evaluator should be welcomed in both roles; but the roles should not be confused, and the scientist has a moral obligation to see that they are kept distinct so that statements of fact are not confused with interpretations of fact.

If no good of life is absolute, if no good is disrelated from any
other good of life, we open the door to moral conflict, for one of
the ways goods of life can be related to each other is through
conflict. If a value conflict is present, then that conflict needs
to be articulated and addressed. When value absolutists enter the
fray, however, as they have done over the abortion issue, positions are advanced that eliminate moral uncertainty and actually, even ironically, render the conflict non-problematic. Two
widely accepted positions have distorted the moral problematic
by so analyzing the abortion issue that uncertainties have in
effect been eliminated. They are the positions that abortion is
murder and that choice is an inviolable right. Both views deny
that abortion is a moral problem. These views represent moral
extremes and appeal to value absolutes to generate positions that
express moral certainty. Unless we eliminate these extremes, we
cannot clear the ground for a morally moderate position.


IF ABORTION IS MURDER . . .

〈 If abortion is murder, abortion is not a moral problem.〉This is
not a controversial claim, but a simple fact of linguistic analysis.
〈 For murder is, as a moral concept, a killing that cannot be
justified〉 To identify an act as murder is to draw a conclusion
about moral meaning and to present a moral evaluation in which
any moral problems involved in a particular killing are finally
decided. And they are decided without qualification. To describe
an act of killing as murder is to pass judgment on the moral
unacceptablity of the killing, no questions asked. No person
familiar with the workings of moral discourse would waste time
discussing the possibility of a moral murder (i.e., an unjustified
killing that could be justified). This would be a nonsensical and
contradictory notion, one not allowed by our moral language.

If abortion is synonymous with murder, then abortion is without question an evil that will allow no extenuating circumstances
or qualifications. It would be folly to argue that abortions could
present a moral problem under this description, because the
identification with murder establishes abortion as a moral evil.

Those who hold that abortion is murder do not have a moral

problem with abortion. They have so described abortion that the moral meaning is unarguably clear. However, it is logically inconsistent to hold that abortion is murder, then to argue that some murders are permissible. Those who hold that abortion is murder—and then also argue that abortions are permissible in the cases of rape, incest, or when a mother's life is in danger—throw logic to the wind: they argue that abortion is by definition an unjustifiable killing, then offer extenuating circumstances that show it is not unjustifiable. "Abortion is murder" is an absolutist position that will not brook exceptions. Persons who hold this view do not have good rational grounds for arguing that abortion is murder and also that it isn't, for the logic of "murder" doesn't work that way. If abortion is murder, it is simply wrong. It is not a moral problem.

## IF CHOICE IS AN INVIOLABLE RIGHT . . .

The second absolutist position that undermines the claim that abortion is a moral problem is the view that all abortions are morally permissible. If this is so, abortion is not a moral problem. Again, the extremity of the position eliminates the moral problematic, for if the fetus cannot be granted any kind of recognition as a being deserving of moral protection, then as long as a fetus is recognized as a fetus, even into the third trimester of pregnancy, even up until delivery, then killing it would be permissible. There would be no such thing as a "trivial" abortion that showed moral insensitivity, like the one proposed by Judith Jarvis Thomson, the philosopher who first argued strenuously for the right of a mother to make decisions about the use of her body. Her example of what I would call a trivial abortion is one requested in a woman's seventh month where the woman "wants the abortion just to avoid the nuisance of postponing a trip abroad."[11] If all abortions are permissible, there is no possibility of a trivial abortion, or one that seems to reflect moral callousness.

And if all abortions are morally permissible, then there is no moral question about the status of the fetus. What that means is that up until such time as personhood status is acquired, and that necessarily would be at or after delivery, a fetus is to be granted no status other than that of a developing and living tissue. The act of forcibly expelling a fetus from the uterus and either allowing it to die or actively killing it—up until the time of delivery—has no more moral meaning than a tooth extraction or the removal of a tumor. It is a biological truth that something can be produced by a species without being considered a member of that species. If all abortions are morally permissible, then the life of a zygote has the same moral worth as that of a full-term fetus the day before delivery—none. Both are simply tissue products.

But the fetus does grow and develop, and some account needs to be taken of the difference between a two-hour-old fertilized egg and a full-term but undelivered fetus. The experience of the mother needs to be integrated into our moral evaluations, for no mother would be willing to say that a full-term but undelivered fetus is of no moral worth. Even the *Roe v Wade* decision takes into account this difference. In fact, *Roe v. Wade* took pains to establish a time frame when the moral problematic seemed so significant that the moral community (or the "state," in legal language) could overrule a woman's right to decide for abortion, restricting that right because of a compelling interest in protecting viable fetal life.[12] When, on the tenth anniversary of *Roe v. Wade*, President Ronald Reagan spoke about "our nationwide policy of abortion-on-demand through all nine months of pregnancy," he completely misled and irresponsibly distorted what *Roe v. Wade* allowed. *Roe v. Wade* states that second-trimester abortions cannot be granted on demand but only in consultation with a physician, and third-trimester abortions, which are exceedingly rare, are restricted to pregnancies in which the mother is facing a dire threat to her life.

If the right to choose an abortion is inviolable and absolute, then taking account of developmental factors and seeking to determine the relevance of certain biological facts to the moral debate becomes meaningless. If choosing abortion is an absolute, and choice is the absolute value to which all other values and facts are subordinated, then any restrictions one might place on abortion would be simply arbitrary and a concession to public prejudice. Those restrictions would not constitute authentic concern for moral ambiguity and uncertainty. If abortion rests on an absolute and inviolable right to choose abortion, the moral problematic drops out—there are no morally callous abortions and even no moral grounds that would prevent a society worried about population growth from demanding and enforcing abortion as a matter of public policy. The objection certain women might have to being forced to abort their fetuses against their will might constitute a protest against social policy, but it would not be an objection where momentous moral issues were at stake. The feeling of a mother toward her developing fetus—of wanting to protect it and promote its welfare—could be attributable to such things as hormonal convulsions or anger at having one's property taken away, as if protesting an enforced abortion had the same moral force as protesting the state's decision to put a sidewalk on a property owner's land for the common good.

If abortions are always and under every circumstance morally permissible, they are non-problematic from a moral point of view. If moral concern did attach, it might be in the social justice sense that the procedure is not uniformly available to all who might want it. But beyond that concern, or the concern that might be expressed for the woman who faces limited physical risks by electing the procedure, abortion would not present itself as a complicated and perplexing moral issue. No ambiguity about moral meaning would arise, and no moral objections would force persons into the agonizing work of moral decision-making.

## SUMMARY

The theory of just abortion is grounded not in a notion of Kantian obligation or utilitarian calculation, but in an understanding of human beings, their relationships, and their moral valuation of certain goods of life. The abortion debate is grounded in value conflicts involving certain goods of life, particularly the preeminent good of life, which is life itself.

The goods of life, I have argued, are relational rather than absolute. A relational view of values holds open the possibility that in the complexity of existence, values that are inherently good and worthy of being promoted can come into conflict with one another. On the abortion issue, moral conflict arises when a pregnancy is determined to be undesirable and unwanted, and the good of life ingredient in pregnancy is challenged by other goods that cannot also be honored if one were to honor the good of life. The relational view of values argued for here, by refusing to honor the good of life as an absolute good, opens the possibility that some pregnancies can be justifiably terminated and a developing form of human life justifiably killed.

In order to open this possibility, I have confronted two positions based on value absolutism that would, if not refuted, prevent my morally moderate position from gaining a hearing. I articulated two extreme but commonly heard positions on the abortion issue: "Abortion is murder" and "Choice is an inviolable right." Both of these positions express the idea that the moral meaning of the life developing in a human pregnancy is self-evident and beyond controversy, so that the moral meaning of abortion in either case also is self-evident. I have not explored specific reasons for the positions at issue in each perspective. Neither have I identified any particular individual or group with either perspective, for that is not crucial to my case. I have only wanted to show that value absolutes eliminate moral problems, and that advocates of either of the extreme positions articulated above are committed logically to the position that abortion is not a moral problem. If these extremes are not exposed as committing persons to logically rigid, even fanatical, positions that can be tempered and qualified only on pain of contradiction, the idea of exploring a non-absolutist position on abortion cannot even get under way. And my purpose in this book is to argue for a non-absolutist view of abortion on the grounds that the moral meaning of abortion is complex rather than simple, and problematic rather than reducible to clear-cut, absolutist positions.

The theory of just abortion requires that we first establish that abortion is a moral problem. Moral problems are created whenever human beings act to violate the goods of life, and abortion is morally problematic because something universally recognized as good—the good of life ingredient in pregnancy—is willfully destroyed in the course of the abortion procedure. Yet, because that good of life is not to be honored independently of other goods, because it is not an absolute good that by definition could *never* be justifiably violated, we establish the foundation for a morally moderate position on abortion, which at this point would at least open the possibility that the killing of a developing form of human life can be justified and is certainly not to be dismissed tout court as a moral impossibility. I have not yet shown how that justification could be satisfactorily constructed, nor specified the conditions that have to be met to justify such a killing. The first task has been to challenge absolutist views that would prevent even the possibility of a morally moderate argument from getting off the ground.

Having rejected value absolutes, however, we then confront the task of reconsidering life and how it is to be valued. Even though life is now to be considered a value in relation to other values, that view does not permit us to devalue life or dishonor it. The good of life must still be so valued that it maintains its formidable position as a universal and basic good of life that is both intrinsically valuable and even preeminent among the goods of life.

But having rejected absolutism, we can fairly ask, If life is not an absolute good, then on what basis can one decide to honor life at all? Doesn't denying the absolute value of life commit one to moral relativism—that is, to the view that goods and values are simply the products of social systems; that goods can vary from one society to another, one community to another, one subjective individualistic opinion to another; and that no universally acknowledged standards of moral behavior and valuation can be said to hold? We can make this question even more concrete with respect to the abortion question. If 7 million abortions are performed in Russia every year and those numbers indicate social sanction of abortion, by what right does anyone who is not Russian stand outside that particular context and criticize by imposing moral judgments on the Russian attitude toward abortion? Who is to say that there is anything wrong with such high numbers of abortions? This is the relativism thesis that is often provoked when one rejects the value absolutism thesis.

As I have rejected the absolutism thesis, I also reject this relativism thesis: that is why I have grounded this discussion of abortion in the goods of life. For whatever particular individuals, groups, and cultures might think about abortion, one can find universal evidence that life itself is regarded as a good. This holds true even in locales with high numbers of abortions, such as Russia.[13] Holding the good of life to be absolute would invite a dangerous fanaticism ultimately destructive of the value of life, as I have tried to show; but falling into relativism would lead inevitably to moral incoherence, since ultimately no good could command any respect as a universal good. There would be only the good you hold to be good, and the good I hold to be good, and no standards for valuation, either positive or negative.[14] A true moral relativist would have no grounds for establishing what is good beyond his or her own arbitrary and subjective decision: one might even conceive of individuals who reject the thesis that life is a good, and who operate accordingly;[15] or who find themselves unable to summon reasons to criticize such morally abhorrent practices as racial apartheid, ethnic cleansing, performing clitoridectomies on young girls, torturing of political prisoners, and so on. Ethical relativism prevents the extension of moral judgment beyond the group and, ultimately, beyond the individual who offers it. If absolutism is dangerous, relativism also is dangerous. Grounding the moral life in universally respected goods of life subverts both absolutism and relativism. The moral life people actually live, where conflicts actually arise, is never quite so clear as these alternatives suggest.

In order to articulate the moral conflict that renders abortion a moral problem, I now turn to a reconsideration of how we value life and honor that valuation of life in our existence together as members of a moral community. My case is that in the moral life, we so honor the good of life ingredient in pregnancy that we presume pregnancy to be good, and that articulating that simple moral presumption is essential for understanding how it is possible to justify an abortion, which obviously challenges and even violates that presumption.

Having established the good of life to be good, though not absolutely so, I will now briefly examine what I am calling "moral presumptions." Abortion challenges a particular moral presumption about the value of life. This presumption ought not be equated with an absolute value, for as a presumption it does not hold in all cases. Yet neither is it a relative value, since it is a presumption universally shared. It is in relation to a moral presumption regarding the value of life that we will derive the specific conditions that will allow us to argue for the idea of just abortion.

# 2

# The Moral Presumption at Issue in Abortion

Working toward a theory of just abortion requires first that we understand something about moral presumptions and how they function as regulative action guides in the moral life. Only then can we articulate the particular moral presumption at issue in the moral controversy over abortion. When that presumption is in place and its force recognized as operative in the moral life, we can take the next step and identify the conditions that would have to be met if we are going to lift that presumption and morally justify a particular abortion.

## MORAL PRESUMPTIONS: FOUNDATIONS FOR THE MORAL LIFE

### MORAL PRESUMPTIONS IN ACTION: BELIEFS AND VALUES

A theory of just abortion cannot be generated out of nothing or in relation to nothing. It cannot be an arbitrary construction. If it were, we would find no basis for accepting it. It would make no appeal to us; it would fail to reflect the presence of a common ground for our moral life in community.

A theory of just abortion—a theory that attempts to establish conditions that would justify an abortion—is generated in relation to a particular moral presumption regarding the good of life ingredient in pregnancy. Moral presumptions are not often talked about in ethics, and the term may seem unfamiliar, even intimidating. The lack of attention given to moral presumptions by professional moral philosophers may lend weight to our initial resistance to see the important role that these presumptions play in how we conduct ourselves in our common life. I pause to investigate this issue not to propose new ethical theory, but to point out a feature of moral life that is always present and expressing itself in our moral relations and practices.

I'll begin by offering a short description of what is meant by a moral presumption. A moral presumption embodies a vision of the good, the right, and the fitting; it defines the springs of action that are constitutive of moral selfhood; it expresses itself in the principles that regulate our common life in community; and it manifests itself in operational norms of everyday action and decision-making.

Moral presumptions define widely accepted standards of action and behavior that people use and rely on when they act consistent with communal values. Referring to communal values is, admittedly, redundant, for values are not simply interests and tastes, which can be quite subjective and individualistic. Values, rather, are always communal: they are public in that they are standards transcending individual taste, carrying a claim to be recognized by the community. They can be discussed, analyzed, ordered, and justified in rational discourse. A meaningful discussion about values presupposes a common lifeworld, a shared cultural context in which persons respect one another and care about ideas and values as determinants of their life together.[1]

The values enshrined in moral presumptions form the bond of unity for moral community, for it is in moral community that persons are respected by virtue of being persons; that they treat others justly and expect fair treatment from others; that they come to understand themselves as committed to a vision of the good life and a hopeful future on the basis of beliefs, traditions, values, practices, purposes, ideals, and hopes that they share with others. We have created forms of rational discourse that allow us to structure a moral language about values, and we use this discourse every day to construct moral meaning in our world and to express our being as moral selves.

Moral presumptions do not necessarily provide pat answers to every morally challenging issue that arises. Rather, they function to embody ideas of goodness: they serve to guide us in the everyday course of events, providing the magnetic force by which we navigate as moral agents in a complex, conflicted, and often ambiguous moral universe. Although we do not typically reflect on moral presumptions, we do employ them, appealing to them whenever we act, whenever we reflect on the meaning of human action and the beliefs and values that action inevitably expresses. We can say that as moral persons, we embody our moral presumptions and act consistently with them; and it is certainly within our power to subject these presumptions to analysis and reflect on them critically, as we do whenever we engage in the work of moral philosophy, whenever we explain our justification for an action, seeking to conform that action to a shared idea or vision of goodness. Yet moral presumptions are more often than not a silent accompaniment to action. We do not typically or ordinarily reflect on them, then apply them to a situation. Rather, they reveal their presence whenever we act immediately and intuitively in the direction of the good, which is to say that they are present unconsciously.[2] Referring to them as presumptions draws attention to the fact that we may very well not be aware of them.

Moral presumptions, in sum, are embodiments in action of deep-seated and shared beliefs and value commitments. They serve to locate persons in the ethical space of moral community. They express our moral attitudes and direct our attention to shared visions of goodness and action aimed at enhancing and promoting the various goods of life. Whether articulated or not, they manifest the core values and vision of good life through which human beings construct the foundations of moral community. When they are articulated, moral presumptions express our moral interpretations of human action and locate us in a moral universe. They disclose our moral commitments, and they identify the values and beliefs we actually enact in the world.

We can infer moral presumptions from our actions. Whereas moral principles can be abstracted from action—they can be debated; they can be affirmed or denied; they may reflect one's actual moral relations or stand over against them—moral presumptions are always enacted. Moral principles provide one means of articulating the meaning of moral presumptions, and from that articulation we derive moral rules and principles that articulate prescriptions about what to do and how to act. Moral principles uphold the goodness of truth-telling, of keeping promises, of protecting the helpless, while condemning actions that are harmful to self and others. The expression of a moral principle, however, is contingent with respect to action—that is, one may or may not enact the moral principles one articulates as one's own. A moral presumption, however, is based on beliefs that are themselves expressed in action, and every action reveals the beliefs and values that comprise the moral presumption.[3]

A moral presumption against suicide, for instance, may be articulated in a moral principle that says, "Killing oneself is wrong, for this is to treat oneself as a means to an end" (the end being, say, elimination of pain). When the moral presumption against suicide is enacted, persons who are in pain or turmoil that might lead them to consider choosing suicide do not act or even think in such a way that suicide offers a prospect for dealing with life issues.

Violating a principle that suicide is wrong leads one to acknowledge that suicide is abhorrent and irrational, and because the principle does not usually articulate exceptions—or acknowledge them—principles lead to absolutist prescriptions (i.e., "Suicide is never justifiable and one ought never to commit suicide"). But if what we confront is a moral presumption against suicide, rather than a principle, we see people actually honoring the presumption by how they regard the care and security of their persons. It's not so much that we see them refusing to drive on bald tires after drinking alcohol (the moral presumption there is not technically suicide-related, for there is no reason to impute a suicide motive to a drunk driver on bald tires), but that we see them concerned about emotional or psychological states (e.g., depression) that might lead persons, either themselves or others, to consider suicide seriously. Observing the moral presumption against suicide is operational in everyday life, so that emotional setbacks, interpersonal conflicts, and stresses of one sort or another do not lead persons to consider suicide as an allowable solution to these common problems. However, given its status as a moral presumption and not an absolute prohibition, the presumption against suicide opens the door to the possibility of a rational suicide, a self-killing that is morally justifiable.

The beliefs and values that are affirmed in seeking to honor the moral presumption against suicide are enacted and avowed, and their force is felt most keenly when one considers the possibility of lifting them for an exception to the presumption against suicide, which one would consider as a way of seeking to promote goods and values that cannot be promoted simply by following a moral principle uncritically, as if it were a moral absolute. What stands in the way of suicide for a person who has been told a medical condition will prove fatal and that the death will be slow and painful, and that it will cause great distress to loved ones, is the moral presumption against suicide. So deeply is this presumption honored—sometimes in principle—that even so bleak a medical prognosis as sustained intractable pain is, for many, insufficient cause for lifting that presumption. Not committing suicide in such a situation means something other than the fact that one is continuing to follow a moral principle that says suicide is wrong, abominable, and irrational. It means that one has not found sufficiently good reason to overrule a moral presumption against suicide.

If it be true that moral principles underlie our everyday actions, it is also true that moral presumptions underlie moral principles themselves. Moral principles are rational articulations of value commitments and beliefs about how the moral life should cohere with our visions of what is good and right and fitting, and it is that presumption of belief and value that manifests itself in action, that allows one to impute a particular moral meaning to action, whether or not that interpretation of moral meaning corresponds to the agent's own understanding.

## MORAL PRESUMPTIONS AND COMMUNITY

Although moral presumptions are manifest in the actions and behavior of individuals, and express individual commitments to values and beliefs, they are decidedly social constructions. This can be seen in the fact that moral presumptions reveal our character, which identifies the way in which persons have been formed in moral community and are predisposed to act in the world.[4] And they function as the practical guides to action that members of a moral community put to work in their daily lives.

As I have already discussed, moral presumptions are more relied upon than thought about. Without much reflection we put them to work in all kinds of situations and circumstances not only to help us decide what to do but to shape our interpretations of moral meaning as we seek to comport ourselves in the world in a way consistent with our deeply held beliefs and value commitments. Our moral presumptions will always indicate who we are (character, being) as well as what we do (action). The same will hold true about moral presumptions in community. Considered socially and politically, moral presumptions embody the bonds of unity—the ideals of moral practice, the practical guides to action, the shared values and social conventions, even the bond of a common moral language—that create identities for moral communities and that hold them together.

We acquire our moral presumptions from our life together, through our engagements with social institutions and community influences—from parents, families, teachers and educational systems, religious communities, political organizations, and from all that a society does to help individuals develop a shared sense of historical and social identity. So important is social context for moral formation that we must conclude that it is not reason that leads us to accept the values we hold and to which we are committed, but that it is the acceptance of socially constructed and transmitted values that defines the limits of what we hold to be reasonable.

Within a moral community, moral presumptions are widely shared. Common commitment to particular values helps to create social identities while fostering moral cohesion in the society as a whole. In a pluralistic society, however, where a variety of smaller, primary communities exist within larger, more inclusive and extensive communities, some differentiation may appear in the values that individual communities emphasize. In a pluralistic society, individuals often belong to several communities of value—those that are primary and involve face-to-face relations, and those that are extensive and transcend those primary relations in the name of more inclusive values.

One need only look to the American social scene to see the differences that emerge in the pluralism of moral communities. Primary communities transmit definite practices and attitudes that distinguish them from others in regard to a variety of issues, including such things as how authority is to be respected; obligations toward parents or the elderly; the extent to which education is honored; how racial or religious intermarriage is received; the role of religion in directing family life and community norms; and drug and alcohol use. How a college fraternity as a primary community would (or might be expected to) place positive value on alcohol use as a bond for social unity will differ dramatically from the moral meaning attached to alcohol use by a temperance group or organizations dedicated to alcohol abstention (e.g., Alcoholics Anonymous); and both of those primary groups could be at odds with the values honored and promoted by the extended and inclusive moral community. That extended community could be expected to make room, through law and social sanction, for a more inclusive and plural environment where many views could be presented simultaneously, a community that would transcend two such smaller communities in conflict with one another by making room for both.

Because individuals can belong to more than one community and the values important to one community can come into conflict with those of other communities, any particular moral perplexity or value conflict may turn out to be a conflict between the moral presumptions of the communities themselves. When that happens, the bonds of unity that sustain and preserve one's moral identity in community are threatened. Psychic discord can result for individuals who experience such a conflict. Consider the case of the person who wants to observe, say, a principle of responsible behavior with respect to practicing artificial birth control, who sees doing so as a good, and who receives from the extensive community of which he or she is a part support for valuing birth control and for practicing what is deemed to be, in society, responsible behavior. Suppose that this same individual happens to be a member of a moral-religious community that promotes the good of openness to natural procreation and pro-hibits artificial birth control as subversive to that good. The individual would likely experience perplexity and conflict about the meaning of responsible behavior with regard to birth control.

But even if persons caught between opposing moral systems are able to resolve their individual psychic discord by allowing the interpretive structures of one community to overrule those of another, thus allowing one moral presumption to resist the chal-lenge of its opposite, deep social discord can still result. The moral community that seeks to advance and protect its moral presumptions in a larger, pluralistic society does not find itself opposed only by another moral presumption, but by an opposing moral community, with the result that social fractures open in the larger pluralistic society itself. This, I would argue, is pre-cisely what has occurred in America over the abortion issue. The "clash over absolutes," as it has been termed, is actually a con-flict between two communities that have sought to embody opposing moral presumptions and that, in the process of po-litcal debate, have lost sight of the derived nature of their presumptions. In defending the moral presumption of their community, proponents on both sides have absolutized the moral presumption adhered to in their community—and thus lost sight of the moral problem that had originally challenged them to confront the interpretive ambiguities and moral com-plexities of the abortion issue as a conflict between moral pre-sumptions.

Moral presumptions may appear to members of a moral com-munity to be objective truths, those unchanging moral realities that establish certainty for one's moral identity both individually and in community. But moral presumptions are not objective truths in the sense that disagreement with them would necessarily indicate irrational and delusional behavior; and they cannot be acquired independently of community affirmation and interpretation. Becoming aware that our moral presumptions are derived from our moral communities need not force us to see those values to which we are committed as merely relative or lacking in moral foundations, but such awareness can help us to resist construing the values to which we are committed as being absolute. They cannot be absolute since they do not exist independently of the persons who hold them or of the communities that honor and promote them.

When we reflect on and even confront the moral presumptions we have appropriated through our particular moral communities, we position ourselves to understand our moral presumptions *as* presumptions. We position ourselves to evaluate critically the most honored and cherished of our value commitments, the purpose being not to deny them but to affirm them as values understood and freely accepted. Self-conscious critique of our value commitments exposes us to their social character—to their status as derived from and through community—and to the danger of absolutizing any particular moral presumption. That danger is simply that once a moral presumption is absolutist it can no longer take into account the particularities of circumstance and the uncertainties of the situation where moral conflicts arise in the common life. Absolutizing a moral presumption necessarily orders the world in a way that does no justice to the complexity of the world or the moral life itself. And not least among the casualties in the absolutizing process is the loss of a common moral discourse, for interpretive disputes and disagreements, rather than being based on a common general framework, are reconstructed to posit one closed system of moral reality against another closed system. Conversation breaks down—and when language doesn't work, one opens the door to the threat of violence. The loss of a common discourse means that what is sought is not conversation, but conversion; and conversion often relies on coercion.

## MORAL PRESUMPTIONS: AN EXAMPLE OF HOW
## THEY FUNCTION

Let us consider how moral presumptions function, using an example relevant to the abortion debate: promise-keeping.[5] This discussion will lead us to consider the particular moral presumption at stake in abortion.

### The Example of Promise-Keeping

Persons committed to the moral life do not agonize about whether they should keep the promises they make. When we sign contracts or make agreements to do what we have pledged to do, we indicate that keeping our promises is something we value, something we know our moral communities value and expect us to honor. In the uttering of a promise we perform the work of promise-keeping, thereby expressing our belief that promise-keeping is good and valuable and that we are disposed to keep any promises we actually make.

Promise-keeping is an example of a moral presumption. We may enshrine our moral thinking about this presumption by fashioning a rule or principle: "One should keep one's promises." Some people may think about promise-keeping as a kind of objective reality since it is widely accepted and could be affirmed by people from different cultures and social contexts.

But promise-keeping is a socially derived moral presumption. Moral communities invest this presumption with importance and direct moral formation with the goal that people who grow and mature morally will honor the value of promise-keeping, believe in the goodness of it, and appropriate it as a moral presumption in their social dealings so that observing the practice of promise-keeping will constitute an expectation of an individual's character.

Persons committed to the moral life do not honor the breaking of promises, do not as a matter of course break promises, and don't expect others to do so. Moral persons do not usually spell out or articulate this understanding of promise-keeping, even though they may take care to clarify what it is they are promising. Belief in the goodness of promise-keeping is not abstracted for reflection, but relied upon and assumed—or, more accurately, *presumed*—as a value that promotes human welfare and the quality of life in community. Promise-keeping is a social and moral institution, something we believe in and value, something to which we are committed and which we want others to honor.

Promise-keeping, in sum, is a moral presumption of foundational importance for individuals in moral community. It would be hard to imagine a community of any sort, either a primary community of face-to-face relations or an extended, transcending community, that did not honor this particular value. In moral community, persons see to it that other members of the community come to honor the value of promise-keeping, that they come to believe in the goodness of it and develop into persons committed to it and disposed to keeping any promises they make. Honoring the promises one makes is one specific way persons can promote and protect the good of practical reasonableness. Promise-keeping helps people maintain friendships and meaningful social relations, all of which could be adversely affected if they were to acquire the habit of breaking promises. Keeping promises promotes the basic goods of life; and performing the work of keeping one's promises actually expresses the fact that promise-keeping is a moral presumption persons believe in and are committed to—and can be expected, as a matter of character and social membership in a moral community, to enact.

## When Conflict Arises

It is not as a principle but as a practice that the moral presumption involved in the keeping of promises is manifest. In our practical transactions with other persons in the common life, promise-keeping is a value to which moral persons commit themselves. Occasionally, circumstances arise that make breaking a promise a possible, even preferable, action, since in the situation presented breaking a promise would promote or preserve other cherished values. But when that happens, persons find themselves confronting a moral problem. To contemplate acting in violation of a moral presumption is not a simple or easy thing, for one's moral presumptions are one's own beliefs and value commitments, one's preference to be a person of a certain sort—in this case, a person who keeps promises. In order to justify breaking a promise, persons in such situations will have to determine whether they can justify an exception to their own preference to act in such a way that they honor the moral presumption of promise-keeping. To confront a situation where one's moral presumptions are challenged is to experience a moral problem, for one cannot now simply act on the presumption but must face the prospect of acting against it.

At this point, the person confronting a moral problem must articulate the presumption under challenge and determine if there are good reasons to lift that presumption. It is agonizing to face such situations, for most of our encounters with others do not provoke such conflicts. We presume that we should keep our promises, so that when we make a promise we typically and simply act in accordance with our presumption—that is how a moral presumption works.

Individuals may face a situation where breaking a promise seems to be the only way to preserve other important values. In these situations of moral conflict, the individual will grasp that the presumption against promise-breaking is not absolute and that holding to it absolutely would present problems for other moral presumptions that are seen as more important in this particular situation. But the conflicted individual will conclude this only in the light of a compelling moral reason that is, finally, sufficiently weighty to justify overturning—lifting—the moral presumption against breaking promises. When, in situations of moral conflict, persons decide to act contrary to an accepted moral presumption, they only do so in relation to that presumption. That is, the presumption is not disavowed or its influence denied, and its presumptive claim on moral outlook and behavior is actually acknowledged in the interpretive act whereby the presumption is lifted. A moral presumption is a barrier to any action that would oppose it, even in a specific and singular circumstance.

Justifying an exception to a moral presumption about promise-keeping would be unnecessary were the presumption not ordinarily determinative of action. By confronting our moral presumption and considering the reasons that might allow us to override the presumption in a particular situation, we are affirming the status of the presumption as a presumption. A peculiar circumstance has arisen wherein acting in accordance with a moral presumption is not obviously the good, right, and fitting thing to do, for other presumptions that are also important or perhaps even more important than the presumption about promise-keeping are at stake in the conflict. The conflict serves to make us aware that we are committed to the good of promise-keeping, and that we shall continue to hold it as a moral presumption, although we do so aware that it is a presumption and not a value absolute that will brook no exceptions.

So deep do our moral presumptions go that finding a circumstance and a justification sufficient to overturn our commitment to keeping promises, or telling the truth, or preserving human life is—and should be—difficult. Yet conflicts do arise. A case familiar to students of ethics is that of a murderer pursuing a victim along a street. The victim tells a bystander where he is going to hide from the pursuer. The murderer stops to inquire if the bystander knows the intended victim's whereabouts. The problem the student faces is this: does the bystander tell the truth, thereby possibly contributing to the death of an innocent person? Or does the bystander lie, thereby violating a moral prohibition against lying?

A moral absolutist would say that the prohibition against lying allows no exceptions, so lying to the pursuer is not permitted. Immanuel Kant, the foremost proponent of deontological or duty-based ethics, said just this. Kant saw no moral conflict in this case; in fact, he devised this case in an essay entitled "On a Supposed Right to Tell Lies" just to make the point.[6] Since in Kant's analysis lying is wrong in that it shows disrespect "to men in general"—it subverts the foundational value of truth and treats persons with a fundamental disrespect, as if they were not worthy of being told the truth—morality demands that persons not lie. Lying is wrong even if the consequences do not appear immediately harmful. Kant's absolutism strikes many persons as harsh and insensitive, and clearly our moral intuitions are such that most of us would tell the lie to save the life—and probably without too great a pang of conscience. This case presents a conflict between moral presumptions: the good of truth-telling is pitted against the good of acting to preserve an innocent person from a murderous attack. So strong is the latter presumption that it would constitute an allowable and justifiable reason for overturning another moral presumption we hold dear—the moral prohibition against lying.

The relevance of this discussion for the abortion issue is that if we consider abortion to be a moral problem, then abortion must be justified in relation to, and in opposition to, a moral presumption. Is there one or more than one moral presumption at issue in abortion? What are those moral presumptions? Is abortion a conflict over opposing moral presumptions, or have we allowed our social policy dispute over abortion to obscure the moral problem at the heart of the issue? What precisely is the moral problem at stake in abortion—and in relation to which moral presumption(s) does it arise?

## THE MORAL PRESUMPTION AT ISSUE IN ABORTION

The contemporary abortion debate is sometimes construed as being a conflict between two moral presumptions, each of which reflects deeply held dispositional beliefs and value commitments, and each of which is supported and sustained through its respective moral community. However, a closer analysis of the moral issues reveals that there is only one moral presumption at stake in abortion.

### RIGHT TO LIFE

In the theory that abortion involves a conflict between two moral presumptions, one of those presumptions accepts the view that fetal life is to be valued and honored as if the fetus were a fully incorporated member of the moral community and deserving of the protections that possessing a right to life—which all members of the moral community possess—affords. The moral presumption that accompanies this view of fetal life is the one expressed in the abiding concern for preserving, protecting, and promoting the good of human life. Procreation is a natural expression of that good, which is basic and foundational. While pregnancy constitutes the biological process whereby persons act to honor and promote the good of life, abortion is construed to violate that good because it terminates the life of members of the moral community—fetuses—without compelling moral justification.

In this view pregnancy is a natural consequence of pursuing the good of life itself. The fetus has positive moral value in that it is a product of human persons seeking to promote the good of life; and by virtue of its status as related to the most basic of all human goods, it is accepted into membership in the moral community. The fetus is itself not an aggressor, neither does it pose any kind of intrinsic threat to other members of the moral community. It is considered an innocent whose helpless condition demands societal protection against those who would do it harm by aborting it. The killing of a member of the moral community who is both defenseless and of no threat to others would, all things being equal, constitute an unjustified killing, which is the reason why those who oppose abortion—who oppose, that is, the killing of a conceptus/fetus—are willing to call it murder. Murder, as I have already indicated, refers to a killing that cannot be justified.

In the public arena, this moral position has sought to focus the issue at stake in abortion on the overriding claim that a conceptus/zygote/embryo/fetus can make as a member of the moral community. The argument advanced and defended by advocates of this moral position is that the fetus is a person—that it is, for reasons having nothing to do with its biological stage of development, deserving of membership in the moral community. That status is conferred from the moment of conception; and because the fetus holds that moral status, it possesses a right to come to term without being aborted. This constitutes a moral description of the so-called right to life position.

Reproduction—pregnancy—is therefore recognized in the moral community as a means of promoting the basic good of life. With this moral presumption in place, one is positioned to value pregnancy as good and the process of human reproduction as desirable.

Given this moral presumption, action aimed at protecting the right to life of members of the moral community, which includes the human person at even the most elementary form of biological development (i.e., the conceptus or zygote), is morally required. It is required because life itself is the most basic good persons can possess, and the moral community must see to it that persons are not deprived of this good. This good of life is so basic, and the moral presumption that it is good so foundational—life being the condition necessary for acquiring all the other goods of life—that defending the fetus' right as a member of the moral community to life itself suffices to withstand most challenges to its primacy—certainly the challenge that comes to it from a mother seeking an abortion. Abortion, in this view, is not permissible, for the claim a woman might make to choose abortion as an exercise of her right to reproductive freedom, while important, is insufficient to withstand the most basic claim human beings can make, which is that they be allowed to live without threat of being deprived of life for non-compelling reasons.

Many right to life advocates would hold that in certain medical difficulties (e.g., a cancerous uterus, ectopic pregnancy), a fetus, through no fault of its own, can pose a threat to the life of the mother—her right to life, if you will. The fetus' right to life is then counterbalanced by the mother's. In this circumstance, many would hold that the fetus' right to life no longer enjoys primacy because it is balanced not by a right to reproductive freedom, but by a morally equivalent right to life—that of the mother. For many in the right to life camp, it follows from this positioning that a compelling reason has been established so that an abortion may be permitted. I find this reasoning inconsistent, since the mother, in this view, enjoys no moral status that would allow her life to be more worthy of saving than that of the fetus, were it not possible to save both. The point, however, is that one could argue to a right to life advocate that certain situations might arise to establish those "compelling reasons," so that an abortion would not constitute an unjustified killing (i.e., murder).

PRO-CHOICE

The pro-choice position, which opposes this view, claims that abortion is allowable because the right in question, and the one that assumes primacy, is that of the mother to exercise reproductive freedom. This is the right that can withstand any claim advanced either by or on behalf of a fetus. It is the overruling moral concern that deserves protection, for many pro-choice people hold that the fetus is not an actual member of the moral community—not a person—so that in the absence of a compelling claim by the fetus, the only right at issue is that of a mother who, faced with the tragic situation of an unwanted pregnancy, claims a right to decide whether she shall terminate that pregnancy. The right to reproductive freedom should be protected, these advocates claim, so that a woman confronted with an unwanted pregnancy can proceed should she decide for an abortion.

This view focuses on the right to choose because those in the pro-choice camp have determined that the fetus is not a member of the moral community. The zygote/fetus, therefore, lacks the status to advance a compelling claim. It is not in a position to overrule a decision for abortion made by a pregnant woman, whose moral status is not in question and whose right as an actual member of the moral community to exercise powers of decision-making with regard to her own reproductive life and future is sufficiently weighty to override any claim that would be made by or on behalf of a fetus, which is only a potential member of the moral community.

The moral presumption at issue when a woman faces an unwanted pregnancy is that which attaches to her exercise of choice and reproductive freedom. Freedom to make decisions about one's reproductive life is an acknowledged good of life, one that takes care to apply the good of practical reasonableness to one's desire to act responsibly in participating in the good of reproduction. It is a good of life to be able to exercise control over one's reproductive life, which would mean that one might seek to avoid pregnancy at various times and for various reasons or to seek pregnancy when doing so is desirable—so that one is acting responsibly, and thereby seeking to further the good of practical reasonableness, in relation to promoting the good of life entailed by the biological process of procreation. This exercise of practical reasonableness issues from an actual member of the moral community in relation to a fetus, which is not acknowledged as possessing the requisite moral standing from which to assert a compelling right to life.

The moral presumption at stake in this characterization of the pro-choice perspective is that the right of women who are fully endowed members of the moral community to make decisions about how to exercise their reproductive capacities and thus honor and promote the good of life takes precedence over any claim that might be asserted on behalf of the fetus, whose moral status is not only in question but whose moral standing as a rights-bearing claimant is not recognized and is in fact denied.

## THE CONFLICT BETWEEN TWO MORAL PRESUMPTIONS

Abortion as a conflict between two moral presumptions looks like this: Pro-life asserts the primacy of the moral presumption that life is a good of life to be promoted and protected, and that because the fetus is a person, an actual member of the moral community, its claims must take precedence as the most fundamental right. Behind this view is the reasonable and non-controversial idea that life as a good of life holds a peculiar status since it is the condition necessary for possessing all the other goods of life, so that honoring it is the most fundamental or basic of goods, the one most obviously deserving of protection and promotion in the moral life itself.

Pro-choice, while not denying that life is a good of life, denies that a fetus has moral standing in the moral community sufficient to overrule a woman who, as a fully endowed member of the moral community, seeks to exercise autonomy and her moral capacities with respect to her reproductive life and future. While pregnancy is easily recognized as a good of life, the reality of an unwanted pregnancy requires a mother to consider how she shall act in regard to such a pregnancy; and in the absence of a compelling and overriding claim issuing from the conceptus/fetus, she will honor the good of practical reasonableness, seek to act responsibly in the situation she faces, and exercise her autonomy and decision-making capacities as a fully endowed member of the moral community whose options in regard to the unwanted pregnancy include abortion.

If this fairly summarizes the opposing positions in the abortion debate, then two issues deserve attention. First, it is important to note that the public debate over abortion is framed in terms of incommensurable and competing rights. Rights identify claims that are protected in our political communities. To exercise a right means to claim to be free of anything that would interfere with that exercise. A right to free speech, for instance, is a claim made in the political arena that persons can voice their opinions without undue restraint by political authority. In the American political system, this right is protected by the Constitution, although the right is not absolute—one cannot shout "Fire!" in a crowded theater as an exercise of this right. We sometimes include moral rights in our talk about rights, but the context for rights talk is always political. Even the fundamental or inalienable rights enumerated in the Declaration of Independence are asserted for a political purpose in a very definite political context.

Although a moral justification can usually be summoned for the asserting of a right, rights are not moral assertions per se, although they depend upon moral assessments in the sense that they seek to promote and protect various goods of life. Exercising certain rights may prove morally offensive in particular moral communities, say, on issues like the permissibility of pornography or free-speech protection for racial epithets. Rights may have moral grounding, but in themselves, they identify claims to be free to act in certain ways in one's social and political context. Abortion does involve rights and a right to abortion—but that right is social and political and not in itself strictly moral. It is dependent upon moral judgments—persons who think abortion is immoral do not want to permit people the liberty to exercise that right—but we can lose sight of the moral issue by focusing on the question of rights, which involve a political and social dimension that is, at least in part, something other than a moral evaluation.

Rights and morality are not the same thing. The abortion debate makes this clear. The question about abortion rights issues from determinations about the moral permissibility of abortion, and the social policy debate over abortion is very much a political debate about which right should be allowed to overrule the other when a political community, as a matter of social policy, cannot honor both. In abortion, this conflict is between a right to life claimed for or by the fetus and the right of a woman to terminate an unwanted pregnancy.

An appeal to two distinct moral presumptions is evident in the debate about abortion rights. The presumptions are manifest in the dispositional beliefs and value commitments of those who assert the pro-life and the pro-choice perspectives and who find themselves members of moral communities that have arisen to support and sustain their moral presumption. But the political divide over abortion rights obscures the fact that there is only one moral presumption at stake, and the moral presumption in relation to which the moral permissibility of abortion is to be determined concerns the value of life, not choice. I shall say more about this momentarily. The second issue is this. If abortion is a moral problem, it is so because abortion involves a killing. Life is a good of life; and human reproduction participates in this good as a primary means whereby the good of life is promoted. This constitutes a moral presumption for both pro-life and pro-choice adherents, despite attempts by some pro-life advocates to suggest that those who advocate choice in abortion are actually denying this good as a good, or as a moral presumption.

The disagreement is not over the moral presumption about the goodness of life ingredient in pregnancy, but over the question of whether a fetus, at least up to a certain point in its biological development, should be included in the moral community and receive the protection that many pro-life adherents wish to extend to it. When pro-choice advocates extend their argument to advance a different moral presumption, that pertaining to a woman's right to reproductive freedom, they are not denying the moral presumption of life—they have addressed it and made a moral determination that it does not extend to fetuses. In that, they honor the same moral presumption about promoting and protecting the goodness of life that pro-life advocates honor, although with this difference. Having established that the fetus lacks the moral standing in the moral community to assert the basic or fundamental right of persons to life, the option of abortion appears as a morally permissible exception to the moral presumption about life when an unwanted pregnancy arises. When this exception is articulated in reference to another moral presumption, that regarding the goodness of reproductive choice, it appears that there are two moral presumptions in conflict, and the debate looks to be a debate over apples and oranges. But even for the pro-choice person, the primary moral presumption to be addressed is that which pertains to the goodness of life. What has happened is that a determination has been made about the appropriateness of extending that presumption to an unborn fetus, and in that there is disagreement with the pro-life perspective. The abortion conflict as a moral conflict does not really center on two incommensurate rights, a right to life versus a right to choose, but on whether the fetus possesses sufficient moral status to withstand a challenge the effect of which would be to allow the fetus to be killed. Pro-life says that the moral presumption holds with respect to the fetus, for the fetus is a member of the moral community.

Pro-choice says that the fetus lacks such moral standing. Because the fetus is not able to assume a position of moral standing in the moral community to assert a right of persons not to be killed without compelling reason, the moral presumption about the goodness of life is not extended to it. The presumption is not denied: the point is that a determination is made about the applicability of that presumption. And crude though it may be to make this analogy, that presumption about protecting and promoting the goodness of life is denied to other living things that are not recognized as appropriately belonging to and enjoying full status as members of the moral community—animals slaughtered for food, cancer cells excised or radiated. Pro-choice honors the moral presumption inasmuch as it accepts that reproduction participates in and promotes the good of life, and it is presumed that becoming pregnant is a good thing because of that. But if a pregnancy occurs and circumstances surround it such that the mother does not desire to bring the pregnancy to term, the presumption about the goodness of life and even reproduction does not hold in the light of the fetus' failure to enter into full membership in the moral community. When pro-choice asserts the right of a mother to decide, it does so already having made room for this move by evaluating the claim of the conceptus/fetus to have its life continued and protected and promoted.

The abortion debate, from a moral point of view, is not about a right to life versus a right to choice—it is about a moral presumption that life is a good of life and that bringing pregnancies to term promotes that good. Both sides of the political rights debate agree about this, even if it is hard for them to acknowledge their common ground in a single moral presumption. But that common ground can be seen in both the pro-life valuing of fetal life and in the presumption that pro-choice people make that when a woman gets pregnant, it is good and desirable and everything possible should be done to bring a desired pregnancy to term.

If human reproduction is good and the goodness of it is entailed by a moral presumption, then pregnancy is not controversial from a moral point of view. One can even presume that pregnancy is desirable and that abortion is undesirable. The goodness of reproduction—the beliefs and value commitments persons in a moral community make in affirmation of that goodness—establishes the moral presumption that this good is to be protected and promoted, which is also to say that this moral presumption stands, as a presumption, *against abortion*. To justify an abortion morally, one must confront the presumption against it and argue that compelling reasons exist for lifting that presumption.

By locating at the heart of the abortion debate a moral presumption, room is created for the possibility that, given sufficiently good and compelling reason, the presumption may be lifted in certain circumstances. Lifting the presumption does not mean that one is thereby positioned to deny the force of the moral presumption as it functions in our everyday lives. One's moral argument for allowing an abortion, in fact, must be directed at the moral presumption and engaged with it. One would be seeking a morally justified exception to the presumption.

Arguments for a just abortion will always occur in relation to a moral presumption. Just abortion does not seek to overturn the moral presumption at issue in the abortion debate. It seeks to preserve it and maintain it, although without that presumption being allowed to operate as if it were a moral absolute. Those who confront their moral presumption as a presumption will deny claims that the presumption is an absolute value. In their resistance to absolutism, they will refuse to distort the complexity of the moral life. They will refuse to ignore variables of circumstance that arise in the common life and that persons of goodwill and sensitivity to the needs of others factor into evaluations about what to do and how to act.

One can seek a justification for abortion only in relation to the moral presumption that life is a good of life and that human reproduction participates in that good. The moral presumption involved in the abortion debate is, to be clear, *for life* and *against abortion.*

The moral presumption at issue, therefore, is not "choice," for any woman who proceeds with an abortion ought to have made her decision on the basis of having justified the decision morally. Much of the confusion in the abortion debate today occurs because advocates of choice want to keep the debate focused on issues of political and social rights, when the moral position that would allow them to argue for the moral permissibility of abortion either is not clear, is assumed, or is articulated in language that fails to confront the primary issue as to whether the killing that occurs in abortion can be morally justified. The first step in restoring sanity to the abortion debate will be to acknowledge the common moral presumption that underwrites both the pro-life and the pro-choice positions, which is that life is a good of life and that pregnancy participates in that good and is to be protected and promoted.

A just abortion theory resists efforts to absolutize the moral presumption at stake in abortion. It will establish means by which prospective abortions can be analyzed morally and overrule the presumption against abortion in those cases where the killing that takes place can be determined to be morally justifiable.

## LOOKING AHEAD

On the basis of this discussion of moral presumptions, I will articulate and employ a framework for moral analysis that has a history in the religious and ethical traditions of the Western world. In the next chapter, I shall examine two particular problems to illustrate how this framework of analysis can be applied: the well-known though not always understood theory of just war, and a more recent attempt to establish conditions for removing treatment from severely deformed neonates—a theory of what I would call "just non-treatment of newborns." The process of moral reasoning involved in these two examples can likewise be applied to abortion, and adopting this framework of practical or moral reasoning allows us to restructure abortion not as a moral absolute, but as the moral problem it is. In both cases, the theories will acknowledge the force and applicability of a particular moral presumption. Because the presumption is not absolute, however, the concern will be to ensure the protection of the moral presumption by guaranteeing that stringent conditions are met before lifting the presumption in a particular situation of moral conflict.

# 3

# The Framework for
# Just Abortion

---

Constructing a theory of just abortion requires that we articulate the moral presumption that ordinarily governs our attitudes and behavior with respect to pregnancy and the possibility of its termination. Since pregnancy is a means whereby the good of human life is promoted, we honor the moral presumption that says this good is ordinarily to be cherished, protected, and promoted.

The moral presumption that pregnancy is good entails the view that, ordinarily, we would not have reason to desire the death of a developing form of human life. Neither would it be immediately obvious why a woman who discovered she was pregnant would want to terminate the pregnancy—at least we would not understand this the way we would understand a patient who, upon discovering she had a tumor, would seek a treatment designed to kill the potentially dangerous tissue. The point is that if pregnancy is a good of life, promoting that good would lead us, ordinarily, to protect that life and see that it develops and flourishes rather than to obstruct its development and kill it. That is what the moral presumption against abortion means—and that is how it works: it functions not only to protect the good of life ingredient in pregnancy but also to obstruct efforts to terminate a pregnancy. This presumption is clearly a strong one, and it is supported by strong moral feeling: who would not consider it a grave moral transgression if a woman who desired a child, who was competent and physically fit for pregnancy, was coerced, say, by the state, into having an abortion against her will? Whatever else one might say about such an instance, one can see in that example the strength of the moral presumption against abortion.

Yet for all its strength, the moral presumption against abortion *is* a presumption—it is not a moral absolute. And because it is not a moral absolute, the possibility arises that the presumption can be lifted for compelling reasons.

Articulating those reasons is what a theory of just abortion is designed to do, for a just abortion would be, in a literal sense, an abortion that is morally justified. That is, in fact, the case, since abortion involves the killing of a developing form of human life, and such a killing requires justification, so strong is the moral presumption that ordinarily one ought not to kill a developing form of human life, but honor and promote the good of life ingredient in it.

A theory of just abortion will establish the conditions that must be satisfied if the moral presumption at issue is going to be overruled in a particular situation. If this is not accomplished, then the moral presumption will be understood as having withstood the challenge. The abortion ought not to proceed, for even if legally permissible, it has failed the test of moral justification. But what is that test of moral justification? How do we derive it? Where do we find it?

In this chapter, I offer a defense of the general moral framework that I shall specify as essential to an adequate theory of just abortion. And I want to make certain that my arguments about the abortion issue in the subsequent chapters are not construed as new and innovative. It is important that the framework for moral analysis I am advocating be seen as part of our heritage of moral thinking, even if it is not often articulated as a specific moral approach and doesn't receive the attention we are more

likely to give natural law, divine command, duty-based deontological ethics, or utilitarianism. Just abortion theory begins by
identifying goods of life that are then enshrined in moral presumptions that bind human beings together into moral community. It then articulates a framework and structure for determining the conditions that create a just and morally permissible
exception to a moral presumption—but only on the basis of
having established a moral presumption in relation to which an
exception is sought.

Before tackling the specifics of just abortion I want to explain—and defend—this just approach to ethical analysis as one
that can be—and historically has been—put to work to help
persons determine, in the face of moral problems and value conflicts, whether a moral presumption can be justifiably lifted. The
morally moderate, non-absolutist approach I am advocating can
be illustrated by considering two other morally momentous life-
and-death issues, one having to do with the use of force in the
conflict between nations (just war theory) and the other having
to do with severely disabled neonates.

## JUST WAR

The idea of just war is found in the Western religious heritage.
Christianity, Judaism, and Islam have all tried to develop guidelines for deciding when the use of force in a particular circumstance can be morally justified. The theory of just war received
its most articulate formulation in Christian thought, but it no
longer represents a uniquely Christian perspective. Just war
thinking today forms an accepted framework within which debate over the issues of war and peace, and the use of force, takes
place. Both supporters and critics of the Persian Gulf War in
1991 appealed to it, even in explicit ways, as Vice President
Quayle's speeches about the war as a "just war" attest.

Some of the basic Christian assumptions about the use of force
can still be discerned in today's version of the theory. The theory
affirms ancient Christian commitment to the idea that one ought
not to return evil for evil, and recognizes the duty all of us have

not to harm others. Particular goods of life—including practical reasonableness, the good of friendship, and even the good involved in physical integrity and life itself—underwrite these principles; and these goods all find their way into the moral presumption that resists and even opposes the use of force, especially violent force, to settle disputes between people and conflicts between nations. The presumption of just war theory, therefore, is *against* the use of force to settle conflict. Stringent conditions are set forth to determine whether the proposed use of force in a particular situation can be justified. *All* of the conditions must be met, no war can be considered just that does not meet the conditions, and no war that is not just should be waged.

Although not all ethicists hold to the same list, the following represent generally accepted conditions that must be met if a war is to be deemed just:[1]

- The war must be sanctioned by a legitimate and competent authority;
- The cause must be just;
- There must be a right intention and announcement of that intention;
- Combat or use of force must always be a last resort;
- One must have a reasonable hope of success in going to war;
- By going to war one must preserve values that otherwise could not be preserved.

Additional criteria govern the actual conduct of the war: noncombatants must be protected, and the use of force cannot rely on weapons that are disproportionate to the end of restoring peace. This last criterion rules out everything from dumb-dumb bullets to chemical and strategic (and also tactical, in my view) nuclear weapons.

Given this framework, it is clear why debate occurred over the morality of United States involvement in the Gulf War. On the one hand, the war was sanctioned by proper authority; there was reasonable hope of success; and during the war, military commanders took pains to convince the public that attempts were being made to protect non-combatants while refraining from using inappropriate weapons.

But not all conditions were met. Just war accepts that non-combatants are to be immune from direct involvement in conflict, and that while some casualties might be inevitable, they must be kept to an absolute minimum, with every protection made to safeguard civilians. We learned after the Gulf War that many non-combatants had been killed or wounded, and that the precision weaponry so highly touted during the war did not work as well as had been indicated.[2] Another problem that arose in applying just war theory was that President Bush announced at least three intentions for military action: preserving the "American way of life," stopping aggression, and creating a new world order. These were not morally equivalent reasons, and America's failure to halt subsequent aggression against the Kurds or against Muslims in Yugoslavia (or in Pol Pot's Cambodia in the 1970s) challenges the national commitment to the second. Humanitarian intervention to prevent human slaughter and genocide is always eligible for consideration as a justification for the use of force.

America's failure to clarify a national intention in the Gulf War argued against the use of force, as did the last resort criterion, which arguably was not satisfied before the commencement of hostilities. Many of those who opposed the war, including those in Congress who voted against it, did so on the grounds that the use of force was premature, that economic sanctions needed more time to work. We have learned since that even some of President Bush's top military advisers steadfastly resisted military intervention by appealing to this criterion.

Just war theory establishes a mode of reasoning based on a moral presumption against the use of force. It does not disallow force absolutely, for it is a moderate theory, a theory that holds that sometimes use of force can be justified. It avoids moral absolutism by dismissing those who on one extreme would never, as an absolute principle, use force (pacifists) as well as those who would never entertain serious objections to using force to preserve cherished values—whatever the cost.

Just war theory rejects such extreme, absolutist options. It is morally moderate, and it is put to work in the service of a presumption against using force, which it seeks to uphold and prevent from being lifted. The theory of just war not only acknowledges that war and the use of force can be terrible things, but it attempts to make the use of force difficult to justify. Those who apply it stringently will always find it a reliable ally of peace and justice.

The moral presumption against the use of force and the establishment of those conditions that, if met, would justify a use of force constitute a paradigmatic case for the type of moral reasoning that a morally moderate, just abortion theory seeks to emulate. To underscore the importance of this method of moral analysis in the light of a moral presumption, let us consider one more example.


## JUST NON-TREATMENT OF NEONATES


One of the main reasons abortion presents moral problems is because of the dispute over the point at which a fetus is acknowledged by a moral community to be an actual member of that community and thereby deserving of the protection that all members of the moral community—persons—can rightfully claim, including the most fundamental or basic claim to the good of life itself. Questions about the standing of a fetus in the moral community come to an end, however, once the fetus nears term or is acknowledged to be sufficiently developed biologically to merit inclusion in the moral community. Determining that point in biological development is controversial, for it is on that question that some have argued for person-from-conception on the grounds that the unique genetic makeup of a conceptus is sufficient for determining membership in the moral community. Others have identified other points of biological development, such as neocortical and lung development, organ differentiation, or even the test of fetal viability. Some argue that viability ought to be determined by the current state of medical technology, which would mean that personhood would be extended to the premature baby who is kept alive with the assistance of extraordinary means of life support.

These differences in viewpoint about the meaning and moment of personhood affect how people want the moral community to devise social policy in the light of the moral presumption that promoting life through reproduction is itself a good of life. The moral community faces difficult but legitimate questions concerning the meaning of membership in the moral community; and those questions concern not only the point of viability, but the role of reproductive technologies, and even the moral good of applying extraordinary means to preserve fetal life when resources are scarce and justice concerns might direct medical assistance to other rights-bearing claimants whose membership in the moral community is not disputed.

Despite the questions concerning the fetus' moral status, which is not a dispute over biological facts but an evaluational dispute about the meaning of certain biological facts as they pertain to a fetus' moral standing in the moral community, there is one definite point where such questions no longer arise. Once a live birth ensues, the moral status of the developing human life is usually recognized whatever the medical condition of the newborn.

Reasonable persons in the moral community would not want to advance a case that the kind of debate that has raged over abortion—whether it is justifiable to kill this developing form of human life under certain circumstances—is applicable once a fetus has gone full term, or has survived a premature delivery. The moral community does not seek to justify a willful killing of babies, even under difficult circumstances. Infanticide does not present problems of moral perplexity. Membership in the moral community is granted once a baby is born, so that the killing of an infant, which is defenseless, strikes persons of goodwill as morally abhorrent. The idea that infanticide might be practiced in a particular culture calls forth the judgment that it is morally repugnant and a violation of fundamental standards of moral decency that transcend cultural particularities. The moral status of the conceptus/fetus is problematic; the moral status of the neonate is not.[3]

It is legitimate to ask whether the neonate possesses all the characteristics of a person as members of a moral community understand that term. It is legitimate to inquire into the neonate's ability to exercise its capacities for personhood and to claim, as a member of the moral community, its various rights, including a right to life. But moral communities do not allow such questions to override their presumption that this form of life is good and that the neonate is intrinsically valuable, an end in itself. The moral community extends membership to the neonate, recognizing that its personhood is not yet realized but is, in a functional sense, still potential. Furthermore, this early developmental stage is a necessary condition for fully realized personhood, which lends to the neonate substantive moral standing that the moral community must recognize. What protections and rights the neonate cannot claim for itself, the moral community accepts responsibility to claim on its behalf. The moral community construes the neonate as requiring protection and nurture because of its relative helplessness and developmental immaturity. Recognizing its responsibility to promote the goods of life and to protect and nurture the lives of human persons in their early developmental stages, the moral community affords the neonate protection and seeks to promote its welfare. The moral community regards the killing of a neonate as a most serious matter, one that not only violates law and social policy, but that offends against a deeply held moral presumption that the neonate's life is intrinsically valuable and deserving of societal protection and nurturance.

Moral communities, therefore, even those that may develop social policies that permit abortions, do not approve of infanticide. A society that permitted infanticide would be held in universal moral contempt. The idea of a community refusing to extend protection to the least powerful of its members would be met with moral disdain. The idea of a community denying personhood status to newborns and therefore permitting the intentional and direct taking of the life of a neonate, a baby, is morally repugnant. Even with overpopulation becoming increasingly important as a societal concern, no morally sensitive person is seriously advocating the killing of newborns as a solution to social and economic problems.

Even when we consider cases of medically disabled newborns, the moral presumption is that a live-born issue from a mother, however seriously handicapped it might be, is to be valued by virtue of its status as a human being and its possession of the primary good of life, which is life itself. Moreover, the moral community accepts that a disabled newborn is a person and therefore of intrinsic value. It is accepted as a member of the moral community, even though the moral community recognizes that its capacities for personhood are not fully developed and that some of them may never be functional. Despite this diminished capacity, which the moral community recognizes in newborns, whether disabled or not—and in children, as well as in adults afflicted with various debilitating conditions—no significant disputes arise concerning a neonate's fundamental moral status as person.

When a newborn arrives severely deformed, the moral presumption that the neonate is a person and intrinsically valuable as a member of the moral community disposes members of the community to act toward the newborn consistent with their belief in the goodness of the neonate's life. Their moral presumption falls on the side of seeking to extend care and medical treatment to the disabled neonate rather than on the side of withholding treatment or otherwise acting, directly or indirectly, to see that the baby dies quickly so society is freed of excessive burdens.

But are there ever circumstances when withholding medical treatment to a severely deformed neonate can be morally justified? To ask this question is to raise the specter of a "just non-treatment of neonates" theory. Such a theory would accept the moral presumption that neonates are persons and intrinsically valuable, and it would even acknowledge that the moral presumption at issue stands against withholding treatment.

But the theory of just non-treatment refuses to endorse moral absolutes. As such, the door is open to the possibility that certain conditions in certain situations might prove so compelling

morally that non-treatment of a deformed neonate could be justified.

The degree of medical treatment that should be extended to
deformed neonates has been a topic of much attention, and
medical ethicists differ on many specifics. I want to look at three
medical conditions of such severity that withholding treatment
seems to supersede the moral presumption that one ought to
extend medical treatment to a severely deformed newborn.

The first condition is a rare skin disease called dystrophic
epidermolysis bullosa of the recessive form. Babies afflicted with
this disease can survive until the age of five, but the quality of
their lives is marred by intractable pain, as inferred in the following description: "Repeated episodes of blistering, infection
and scar formation lead to severe deformities, loss of hair, buccal
mucosal scarring, dysphagia, and retarded physical and sexual
development. . . . [T]oe and finger lesions heal with fusions of
digits and loss of nails."[4]

The drug Demaril is given to help ease the pain, but it places
the neonate in a stupor and the pain returns, making such common activities as bathing or dressing so excruciating that victims
scream in anticipation of the pain. Those afflicted with epidermolysis bullosa develop neurologically, but they become suspect
of human touch and distance themselves from human interaction. Ethicist Richard C. Sparks has concluded the following
about this condition:

> The quality of life open to this child is either so irremediably
> pained or else so doped up (relationally non-conscious) that
> should life-sustainers be required or treatment become necessary
> for pneumonia, infections, or other curable diseases, one might
> opt to forgo these efforts in the patient's holistic best interests,
> hoping for ("desiring," not necessarily morally "intending") an
> earlier and easier rather than a belabored and painful dying pro-
> cess.[5]

The quality of such a limited life can be so diminished, and
the condition of constant and unrelieved pain so terrible an
infliction, that a child suffering from this disorder might reason-

ably be denied treatment for other medical problems that could be treated successfully. Such withholding could be considered more humane and life-respecting than allowing a slow and lingering death accompanied by the symptoms of intractable pain. Withholding medical treatment in such a case could be morally justified as in the patient's best interests, and the condition at issue would suffice to allow one to overrule the presumption that one ought to extend medical treatment where it can benefit a patient. The suffering caused by epidermolysis bullosa could be evaluated as so burdensome to the child that it exceeds what a child ought to be expected to bear and what a moral community ought to impose, especially with the child facing death within five years after birth.

A second medical condition that would allow one to challenge the moral presumption that neonates should be extended medical care is hydranencephaly, a condition in which an infant is born suffering from intrauterine hydrocephalus. This means there is no brain present, only tissue remnants of what should have been a brain. These infants have absolutely "no cognitive activity or relational potential. Death is usually imminent within hours, days, or weeks."[6] Given that such infants lack any capacity to enjoy the goods of life in even the most minimal way— they lack an experiential quality of life—the decision to withhold medical treatment, including ventilators and other interim treatments one would ordinarily deliver to neonates suffering treatable conditions, can be justified. These tragic infants lack a capacity for personhood; and the good of life they do possess is robbed of meaning by lack of any possible experiential interaction.

The good of life is not an absolute good, and this condition illustrates why; for without relation to other goods—such as the capacity to experience pleasure, self-consciousness, and meaningful interaction in one's environment—the good of life is insufficient to justify its own continuation. And although not a determinative consideration in withholding treatment, the continued survival of these infants, which on rare occasions has continued for several months, places terrible burdens on caretakers and families. Withholding treatment can be justified as being in the best interests of the patient, who, in lacking a brain, has no reasonable prospect of enjoying even the good of life itself.

Sparks recounts a third situation, the case of Baby Fred. Born prematurely of a severely diabetic mother, Baby Fred suffered low hemoglobin and hematic rates because of the diabetes, and the baby's bowel protruded through the umbilicus. Thirty-six hours of care were required to stabilize the baby after anemia caused fluids to collect in the body cavity. The baby suffered hypoxia, and its blood tended to move away from the lungs in a belated continuation of in utero circulation, which required permanent respirator aid. A seizure ensued, after which an abnormal but not quite flat brain wave appeared. The heart walls were thickened, and the survival prognosis was bleak. Doctors reported that the baby's look when being touched was "anything but happy," and that it seemed to be "pained . . . as if life is not worth living."[7]

Baby Fred suffered so many severe anomalies—brain damage indicating severe retardation, bowel and heart disorders requiring surgery, severe chronic lung disease requiring constant ventilation—that continued medical treatment seemed inhumane. Withholding treatment, Sparks argued, could take the form of identifying the baby as a "no code" so that attempts to resuscitate it would not commence if a cardiac seizure were to ensue, or of allowing it to die by withdrawing the respirator if its condition worsened and no prospect for physiological improvement seemed likely. The life of this baby had become a burden to the baby itself, and non-treatment (cessation of ventilation assistance), Sparks argued, could be seen as best serving the patient's "personal, social and spiritual" interests.[8]

These three examples indicate the kind of physiological disability that could create conditions of such grave severity that reasonable people could consider overruling the moral presumption that affords protection and nurturance to neonates as members of the moral community. These medical conditions expose the presumption that neonates should be treated and nurtured when disabled as a presumption, one for which exceptions can be drawn. The theory of just non-treatment acknowledges the recognition widespread throughout the moral community that the

presumption to care for severely handicapped neonates is powerful and not to be overruled without grave cause. Grave causes
do exist, and the medical conditions just outlined illustrate the
kinds of complications that make overruling the moral presumption a possibility.

Were we to formalize a theory of just non-treatment of neonates, we would have to establish guidelines to help us determine
when we would be morally justified in withholding medical treatment. Such a framework might begin by affirming a moral presumption that neonates, even when severely disabled, ordinarily
ought to be provided with medical care and treatment. That
presumption, however, may be lifted if:

1. The life of the neonatal patient is clearly a burden to the
   infant itself.
2. The intention of withdrawing treatment is to serve the best
   personal, social, and spiritual interests of the patient.
3. The neonate's medical condition is so severe that its pros-
   pects of enjoying the goods of life, including the good of
   life itself, is negligible. There is no reasonable hope that
   the neonate will flourish as a functional human being at
   even the most minimal level, and treatment will, on the
   contrary, contribute to the burdens the patient must bear.
4. The decision to withhold support is kept patient-centered
   and is not determined by the burdens the patient is imposing on others—medical staff, society, and family.
5. The decision is made by those who represent various interests of the patient, including family, physicians and
   medical care personnel, and spiritual advisers.
6. By withdrawing treatment one is trying to preserve respect
   for the good of life rather than to diminish it, and withholding treatment apparently will reasonably accomplish
   this end.

These criteria could be devised and developed other ways, but
this indicates one possible approach to the moral problems
caused by severe medical disability. By construing this theory of
just non-treatment, my purpose has been to show how one would

go about preserving a moral presumption against non-treatment while also recognizing that circumstances might compel one to overrule the force of that presumption in a specific instance.

These criteria establish the conditions under which medical treatment could be justly withheld from a severely handicapped newborn. They support the moral presumption that newborns are ends in themselves—that is, they are members of the moral community whose lives must be protected and nurtured; and the criteria uphold that the decision for non-treatment always be directed toward the good of the patient himself or herself. This approach does not absolutize the presumption. The conditions it imposes function to prevent a decision from being made easily or for reasons that are not patient-centered. The approach provides a framework for evaluation that can be applied to particular situations. Many medical disabilities and anomalies would fail to satisfy these criteria, which would then prevent a moral justification for non-treatment. The three examples given would satisfy these conditions, and non-treatment of these neonatal patients would satisfy the criteria for establishing a course of non-treatment that would be just.

While continuing to support the place of the moral presumption in our moral thinking about newborns suffering severe physiological malformities, this theory of just non-treatment allows for exceptions to the presumption. It is presumed that handicapped newborns should receive medical care and treatment as an expression of the moral community's responsibility for the care of severely handicapped neonates, who are among the least powerful and most needy of its members. Yet that presumption is not absolute. Treatment can be withheld if certain criteria are met, and those criteria are designed to ensure that withholding treatment supports the values embodied in the moral presumption itself. The death of a severely handicapped newborn as a result of non-treatment is tragic, but that death can be morally justified as in the patient's best interest if the moral community establishes criteria that would allow for the overruling of a moral presumption that severely handicapped neonates, as members of the moral community, should be extended care and nurturance.

War is tragic; the death of a severely disabled newborn is

tragic. The theories of just war and just non-treatment of new-borns are not designed to eliminate tragedy but to preserve the good of life. The theories support the moral presumption that life is a good of life and is to be promoted by the moral community. In that regard, the theories stand as presumptions *against* the very activity they make possible, namely, the use of force and the withholding of medical treatment for helpless newborns. Tragic though these actions would be, the greater enemy is certainly the moral absolutism that would refuse to acknowledge that the world is imperfect and that moral presumptions are, in the end, presumptions, rather than absolutes that must be observed with-out qualification. Depriving persons of their powers to analyze situations and employ practical reasonableness would offend against the goods of life and actually deprive persons of their freedom, which is always the problem with moral absolutism. In the end, moral absolutism contradicts the moral life by elimi-nating freedom and the very idea of being an agent capable of some degree of self-determination.

The theories of just war, just non-treatment of newborns, and what I shall now propose as a theory of just abortion are similar in their approach and framework. They eschew moral absolutism in the interest of upholding the connection between human freedom and human moral responsibility; for persons must be free to accept responsibility for their tasks as decision-makers in the complex reality of the moral life, which is life aimed toward goodness and which cannot transpire from one moment to the next except in relation.

# 4

# The Theory of Just Abortion

## FRAMING THE THEORY

Abortion involves a direct and willful killing of a developing form of human life. The moral question is whether or under what circumstances that killing can be justified. A just abortion theory provides the best resource for addressing that question, for among all the approaches to the abortion question today, just abortion is unique in doggedly holding to the idea that abortion always presents itself to reflection as a moral problem.

As I have already discussed, the contemporary abortion debate in America is focused not on the moral issue of abortion per se, but on serious and important social policy issues. The problem is that many of those involved in the social policy debate are advocating absolutist positions on the assumption that the moral issues are clear, non-controversial, and settled. A just abortion theory necessarily challenges the absolutists in this assumption and calls the discussion back to the moral question, which is no longer whether the killing that occurs in abortion can be justified; having eschewed moral absolutism, a just abortion approach is committed to the view that it is possible that at least some abortions can be morally justified. A just abortion approach thus modifies the moral question at issue in the abortion debate to read, "When and under what circumstances is it morally permissible to kill a developing and unborn form of human life?"

A theory of just abortion articulates, in the first instance, the moral presumptions that would ordinarily guide our evaluations and decisions with regard to issues surrounding human pregnancy. A just abortion approach draws our attention back to basic moral affirmations that are, in practice if not always in theory, widely shared in our broader moral community by persons who would consider themselves to be on either the pro-life and the pro-choice side of the abortion question. Constructing a theory of just abortion cannot proceed unless the common moral presumption at stake in the abortion debate has been adequately articulated.

Beyond articulating the moral presumption at issue, a just abortion perspective will specify the conditions and criteria that must be satisfied if one is going to justify lifting the moral presumption that ordinarily holds with respect to abortion. It is tempting to focus attention exclusively on the criteria. But the criteria can only have meaning and relevance in relation to a moral presumption that governs them. It is the moral presumption that generates the moral safeguards—the criteria—that ensure that if the presumption is lifted, it is done in a morally responsible way only for a particular purpose and for restricted causes, then restored to its presumptive status. Just war criteria, for instance, provide the test for morally justifying a use of force in certain situations if various stringent conditions are met, but satisfying the criteria requires that peace be restored and that the moral presumption for settling conflicts without the use of force be in no way subverted.

The criteria that allow for the lifting of a moral presumption in a particular situation are undeniably important aspects of just war theory, but even more important is the moral presumption *against* the use of force that is at the heart of the theory. Likewise, in just non-treatment of neonates, the moral presumption is *against* withholding medical treatment from severely handicapped neonates. And in just abortion, the moral presumption is *against* the willful and direct killing of a fetus. This is a clear statement of the moral presumption governing the abortion question, but since it is also a controversial claim, especially in the light of the fact that just abortion necessarily implies a pro-choice social policy position, its justification must likewise be stated clearly.

## THE MORAL PRESUMPTION AGAINST ABORTION: THE RATIONALE

The moral presumption against abortion holds because life is a primary good of life: human reproduction through the physiological condition of pregnancy promotes that good and is ingredient in it. Generally speaking, pregnancy, although a difficult condition from a medical-physiological and even from a psychological point of view, is, from a moral point of view, a good and desirable condition that is ordinarily recognized as such by the many people who desire to become parents and involve themselves in the care and nurture of children.

I do not find this analysis controversial. Were we to query a typical member of the moral community, and that includes persons on the pro-choice side of the abortion question, we could expect that member to say that promoting the life of the species by reproduction is good. I also believe that typical members of the moral community would affirm the view that participating in family life and assuming responsibility for raising and nurturing children is good, even if certain societal problems (i.e., overpopulation) might cause them to advocate restrictions on pursuing the good, and even if some individuals would claim that this is not a good they choose to pursue themselves for one reason or another. Without compelling reasons to think otherwise, a typical member of the moral community could be expected to operate according to beliefs and value commitments that presume pregnancy to be ingredient in the goods of life and therefore desirable as a human good.

And a developing form of human life is the center of meaning and value in the good of pregnancy. Because it is human and alive, the developing human fetus is to be regarded as good and therefore, ordinarily, deserving of protection. The fetus possesses life, which is a good of life necessary for other goods; and it has already developed sufficiently even as a conceptus to be regarded as a member of the species. To be sure, possession of life and species membership are insufficient to determine that the fetus is the moral equivalent of a person.[1] However, as a practical matter, the moral community does ordinarily grant even to immature and developing human life an incipient moral status, for that developing form of human life is a bundle of potentialities that cannot be realized if what will finally become a person does not pass through the initial and early stages of biological development. Recognizing that progression through those stages is necessary if human beings are going to develop into human persons, the moral community has acted such that it manifests its dispositional belief that such life as the fetus possesses is good and deserving of protection. We see this dispositional belief manifested in the ways moral communities concern themselves with prenatal care, even going so far as to develop social programs to provide medical and nutritional support for pregnant women in need of financial assistance. A fetus need not be regarded as a person to be acknowledged as possessing an incipient moral status; and on this understanding of the moral status of the fetus, it is clear that the moral presumption involved in abortion is that the developing fetus should be protected and nurtured, not harmed and certainly not intentionally killed.

As we have already indicated, the moral presumption at stake in abortion is a presumption *against* abortion. This articulates a general claim that says whenever a woman becomes pregnant, the moral community does not presume that the pregnancy ought to be terminated but, on the contrary, that it ought to continue; and it ought to continue in such a way that the mother and the developing fetus receive care and nurturing and protection from harm. Why? For the simple moral reason that pregnancy is good and desirable. Moral communities acknowledge this good in the moral presumptions that they attach to the good of pregnancy. It is important to note that even in the abortion debate in America, pro-choice advocates have not attacked the moral presumption, which they share with pro-life advocates, that life is a good of life or that pregnancy is, in general, a good and desirable condition. What pro-choice advocates refuse to acknowledge is that all pregnancies are wanted; that all promote the good of life; that the good of fetal life can be affirmed as an absolutely overriding good disrelated to the other goods of life, a good, that is, that can be affirmed without qualification and extracted from the relational matrix of values we discussed in chapter 1. Pro-choice advocates, then, also acknowledge (or should acknowledge) the moral presumption against abortion, but they also hold open the door to the possibility of abortion. They do so not in the interests of subverting the moral presumption against abortion, but as a way of recognizing and articulating the view that the moral presumption against abortion does not hold the status of an absolute moral imperative. It is, rather, a moral *presumption* to which exceptions can be and often are made.

THE IMPERFECT WORLD

One other philosophical commitment shapes just abortion theory and must be acknowledged along with the moral presumption against abortion. That is the recognition that ours is an imperfect world. While no one would reasonably dispute that claim, it is not necessarily clear how the imperfect world factor should bear on a moral analysis of abortion.

A theory of just abortion takes a particular approach to this question. Just abortion theory, like that of just war and just non-treatment of severely handicapped neonates, is premised on the idea that because ours is an imperfect world, doing what is good, right, and fitting cannot always be accomplished by simply acting in accordance with one's moral presumptions. Occasionally, a fully engaged moral response will require persons to confront their moral presumptions as inadequate guides for acting in a particularly difficult or morally complex situation. In an imperfect world, persons are sometimes confronted with situations that lead them to act contrary to their moral presumptions, and when this happens, the decision to violate the moral presumption is not motivated by an evil or perverse will (although that is also possible) but by the person's desire to do good. Persons committed to the moral life will inevitably face such situations— and these situations arise every time a moral problem is provoked and persons find themselves uncertain about what to do or how best to act consistent with the good even though they know how to act consistent with their moral presumptions. For example, I may know how I ought to act so that my action is consistent with a moral presumption against lying—I ought not to tell a lie. But if I face a situation where telling the truth could cost other people their lives, I must decide how to act consistently with the good. Consideration of the good may very well lead me to violate the moral presumption against lying to which I am committed as a member of the moral community.

On the abortion question, a moral problem is generated from the conflict that obtains when circumstances arise in certain pregnancies that call the adequacy of the presumption against abortion into question. Circumstances surrounding a pregnancy can be so complex and incite so many value conflicts and relational entanglements that the pregnant woman may not be able simply to act consistently with the moral presumption against abortion while also acting to honor other values and goods of life.[2]

A just abortion theory, like just war theory, acknowledges that because the world is imperfect, such conflicts are possible. However, the just abortion approach also acknowledges that the moral presumption against abortion cannot be ignored or dispensed with even when a woman elects to have an abortion. *The moral presumption against abortion actually provokes the moral problem of abortion.* Were that presumption neither operative nor normative, no problem would arise in the first place—having an abortion would be the moral equivalent of having a tooth extracted; and the fact that many if not most pregnancies are *desired* indicates that pregnancy is presumed to be a good and desirable condition, morally speaking. The fact that a moral problem does present itself with respect to terminating a pregnancy and killing a developing form of human life indicates that the moral presumption against abortion is continuing to operate and to exert its influence.

· Yet the just abortion approach also takes into account the fact that in an imperfect world, situational complexity requires moral sensitivity. Moral persons cannot always act in accordance with the ideals of action prescribed by the moral presumptions they hold and to which they are committed. Members of the moral community suffer as they face situations that demand morally sensitive responses, as they find themselves thrown out of the complacency and orderliness of everyday existence into a tragic world that defies their attempts to live in that world with a sense of moral certainty. In the tragic and finite world, conflicts cloud our sense of what constitutes right action, and moral decisions are made not so much as expressions of moral certainty but as reactions to moral complexity. And in the face of moral complexity, we are guided not by certain knowledge (i.e., epistemological certainty) but by the visions of goodness that we have developed in moral communities and that motivate us to act, both individually and corporately, not in sure knowledge but in faith and hope.

In a perfect world there would be no conflicts of value, no clouding of moral vision, no disorder in the moral life. This point is relevant to our discussion of abortion because in a perfect world there would also be no abortions. There would be no abortions because there would be no unwanted pregnancies. In a perfect world, none of the circumstances and value conflicts that contribute to a pregnancy being undesirable and unwanted would arise. Truly, every pregnancy would be avowed as ingredient in the good of life and judged desirable because the good of pregnancy would never conflict with other goods. As the Planned Parenthood slogan puts it, "Every child would be a wanted child."

But the imperfections of the world dictate otherwise. It is a sad reality that some women who become pregnant find their pregnancies so enmeshed in practical strife and value conflicts that the good of promoting life cannot be avowed simply or in abstraction from other goods of life. The goods of life, even the good of life itself, are relational goods. In an imperfect world, situations and circumstances may so configure the relations that the good of life ingredient in pregnancy may fail to withstand the challenges that other goods of life, either singly or in combination, put to it. That is why it is certainly possible in an imperfect world for a pregnant woman to de-value the life at stake in her pregnancy relative to other goods and determine that the developing form of life is unwanted and undesirable. In situations of value conflict, even the good of life is subject to moral evaluation in relation to other goods, and some situations may prove so compelling and grave that the good of life itself must be subordinated to other goods so that other cherished and valued goods might be preserved. To recognize this is to shift the moral problem involved in abortion from whether abortions may be morally justified to questions concerning when and how and under what circumstances that justification can be realized.

## THE CRITERIA

Just abortion must be grounded in two essential affirmations. First is the affirmation that a just abortion assumes a moral presumption against abortion; for the idea of a morally justifiable abortion can be constructed only in relation to an accepted moral presumption that ordinarily pregnancies are to considered ingredient in the goods of life, fetal life ought to be protected, and, all things being equal, pregnancies ought not to be terminated and fetuses killed. A just abortion approach provides a moral justification for lifting that presumption in a particular situation of value and moral complexity.

Second is the affirmation that ours is an imperfect world. In a just abortion approach, this affirmation expresses the viewpoint that because the world is imperfect and human beings are fallible, people cannot always enact their moral beliefs and commitments as they would like. Sometimes situations arise that present moral problems, and a fully engaged moral response must take into account not only what action would best conform to one's avowed moral presumption, but also to one's vision of goodness—and these may not always be the same thing. The existence of moral problems and value conflicts is the best evidence we have that ours is not a perfect world, and acknowledging that is to say that human beings are so constituted as finite beings that they cannot possibly achieve moral perfection—in reasoning, in motivation, and in action—even if it is their desire to do so.

Affirming an imperfect world undermines the foundations of moral absolutism. It translates our moral commitments and what we may think to be our moral certainties into moral presumptions. And, when a morally complex situation arises, it allows the possibility that in order to enact a vision of goodness and do the good that one desires, one may have to lift an avowed moral presumption as a fully engaged but also morally sensitive response to that situation.

One other issue relevant to constructing a just abortion approach must be clarified, and that is the recognition that this approach will always be a response to the value conflicts and moral problems created by a particular pregnancy.

It is important to acknowledge that morally speaking, pregnancies are not always, not even usually, biological events that create moral problems. They are just the opposite, and I have emphasized a moral description of pregnancy in which pregnancy is ingredient in the goods of life and acknowledged as such by the broader moral community.

In an imperfect world, the press of situation and circumstance in some pregnancies can induce such conflict or present such serious obstacles to acknowledging a pregnancy as good and therefore desirable that a pregnant woman may decide that were she free to do so, she would not bring the conceptus/fetus to term. If she could wish the conflict away, she would—just as those considering the use of force or the withholding of medical treatment from a severely handicapped neonate would wish their conflicts away. However, a woman experiencing an undesirable pregnancy faces value conflicts that cannot be wished away. The conflicts must be resolved, within certain time constraints, in favor of the moral presumption against abortion or in favor of abortion as an exception to that presumption.

We must be clear that when an abortion is considered and then performed, that abortion is the result of a moral conflict. A woman's desire not to be pregnant is pitted against her own desire to honor the good of pregnancy. The problem is how to act so that one might free oneself of an unwanted pregnancy without unjustly violating the moral presumption that pregnancy promotes life and is ingredient in the good of life itself. Thus the very fact of an unwanted pregnancy establishes the presence of a moral problem, and abortion is a possible response to that moral problem, as is the response of bringing the fetus to term, whether or not the mother gives it up for adoption.[3] The moral problem that arises with the abortion option is not a conflict over the social policy issue concerning the political right to choose abortion versus a fetal right to life,[4] but a conflict over the question of whether or under what circumstances killing a human conceptus (or embryo or fetus) can be morally justified.

Because the just abortion approach disavows in the first instance even the possibility of moral absolutism, it holds open the possibility that in the fallibility and tragedy of human existence, some pregnancies involve circumstances that render them undesirable and unwanted. The press of other goods of life, either specific goods alone or in combination, creates conflict with the good of life involved in pregnancy; and the moral theory of just abortion establishes the conditions that must be met if one is to determine on moral grounds that the moral presumption against abortion can be justly—that is, with moral justification—lifted.

The moral presumption against abortion may be lifted and an abortion justifiably performed if six criteria are met.

## CRITERION 1. COMPETENT AUTHORITY

The abortion must be desired and sanctioned by a competent authority. The primary authority responsible for making a decision to abort a pregnancy is the pregnant woman. Since only women with unwanted pregnancies are logical candidates for abortion, this criterion affirms that the pregnant woman is in a uniquely authoritative position to determine whether her pregnancy is wanted or unwanted. Persons in the moral community other than the pregnant woman may also want or not want the pregnancy to come to term, but generally speaking, it would be morally offensive to coerce a woman who did not want an abortion to have one. Conversely, it would be morally wrong to coerce a woman into having a baby if the circumstances surrounding her pregnancy were such that she was unable to affirm the good of her pregnancy and did not desire to bring a baby into the world. Many women who neither see the good of their pregnancy nor desire to have children nonetheless decide to proceed with the pregnancy and bring the fetus to term. But coercing a pregnant woman into proceeding with her pregnancy against her will presents a serious moral problem, for such coercion means, morally speaking, that the pregnancy has assumed the status of an intrinsically valuable end in itself to which the pregnant woman is being asked to serve as a means. This is to render the woman less than the fetus' moral equivalent. To coerce a woman in such a situation is to treat her disrespectfully, as if she were not a person herself, as if she were not an autonomous moral agent capable of discerning the good and making competent and responsible decisions in relation to her vision of the good.

If the pregnant woman is treated as a fully endowed member of the moral community, as a moral agent capable of acting in accordance with a vision of goodness, then her moral status cannot be devalued over against that of the fetus. Once the pregnant woman is recognized as a person, as an autonomous and competent moral agent, then she must also be recognized as holding a unique and authoritative position with regard to determining whether her pregnancy is wanted or unwanted. A pregnant woman will always consider the desirability of her pregnancy in the context of her social relations and the values of her moral community. Moreover, she will involve others in the process of determining whether she wants to bring her pregnancy to term. For instance, she could be expected to take into consideration the views and counsel of the father (spouse or life partner), family and friends, physicians, and psychological and spiritual counselors. But this first criterion of just abortion requires that the woman's authoritative position to make this determination be recognized.

In the light of this criterion, it is possible that a woman who becomes pregnant by choice may yet change her mind and determine that the pregnancy is unwanted. An unforeseen medical complication threatening the mother's life or promising to result in a terribly malformed and hopelessly pain-inflicted baby could arise and force a woman to reconsider the desirability of bringing to term a pregnancy she had wanted. On the other hand, considering this criterion also allows for the possibility that a woman who becomes pregnant with no desire to do so might decide to bring the fetus to term. This is possible even in the case of rape, where a morally abhorrent and violent act committed against the will and without the consent of the woman resulted in pregnancy. If the moral autonomy of the woman is respected, we allow for the possibility that for various reasons this woman might choose to bring her fetus to term even though many in the moral community would say that in such a situation she is free of any obligation to do so.

A pregnancy cannot be considered a candidate for a just abortion if, in the first instance, someone competent to determine that the pregnancy is unwanted has failed to establish that fact. The first criterion of just abortion rests competent authority in the pregnant woman herself, for she is, if not alone in making her determination, at least uniquely positioned to decide whether the pregnancy is wanted. In certain imaginable circumstances, society could be pressing her to decide that her pregnancy is not wanted when, in fact, she does want it. In other circumstances, she could be part of a society or moral community that wants her to want the pregnancy when, in fact, she does not. The desirability of a particular pregnancy cannot be decided apart from the woman who must go through the pregnancy in the particular circumstances of her life experience. While pregnancy is always ingredient in the good of life, a particular pregnancy may be so qualified by circumstance that the desire to realize the good it contains is diminished relative to other goods, which are also desired. That is to say, the desirability of a particular pregnancy cannot be decided in the abstract, even though as a general rule, pregnancies are to be valued as good and the good of life is usually recognized in the moral community as being sufficient to withstand challenges that value conflicts generate in relation to it.

This criterion does not endorse the view that a woman has a right to do anything she wants with her body.[5] It simply recognizes the pregnant woman as a moral agent who as the legitimate and competent authority must determine whether her pregnancy is wanted or unwanted. If it is unwanted, she remains in a position of legitimate authority to consider the abortion option. Determining that a pregnancy is unwanted is itself insufficient for justifying an abortion, but it is a necessary condition; and this first criterion holds that the pregnant woman herself must be recognized as morally competent and uniquely positioned to determine her own pregnancy's desirability, and that in so doing she should be free of coercion even if, as a member of the moral community, she will evaluate this issue in community and in moral conversation with others.

Legitimate questions can arise about who should decide the abortion question when the mother's competence to make a decision is in question, as it might be in the case of rape or incest, where the mother may be emotionally distraught and psychologically injured, or in pregnancies involving minors or a comatose mother. These are not all equivalent situations, morally speaking, and not all cases would necessarily imply diminished capacity and thereby authorize someone else to make decisions for a woman when she is unable to do so herself. Such cases are best handled on an individual basis, where the particulars of each situation can be fully considered. After all, a pregnant rape victim who is emotionally distraught and decides her pregnancy is unwanted may be no more distraught than another rape victim who might decide to bring the pregnancy to term. And a comatose mother-to-be whose life is threatened by the pregnancy presents the moral community with a situation different from that of a comatose pregnant woman whose life is not so threatened.

Just as the moral community has an interest in preserving a moral presumption against abortion, it also has a responsibility to determine when abortion may be considered in the best interests of mother and society, and possibly even that of the fetus itself. Society is never absent when decisions are made about the desirability of a particular pregnancy, and situations and circumstances can be conceived where society might legitimately play a larger role in directing the abortion decision than it presently does.[6] But generally speaking, a moral community ought not to assume that it can infer all the relevant variables that would go into a particular woman's evaluation of a pregnancy as wanted or unwanted, even when she is unable to do so for herself.[7]

The woman is the person most intimately and directly affected by the experience of pregnancy. Accordingly, the moral community ought to defer as far as possible to her and acknowledge that it is the woman who holds the legitimate and authoritative position on the question of whether a pregnancy is wanted or not. And it is on the basis of that determination that the woman then moves with moral justification into a position to consider the abortion option.

## CRITERION 2. JUST CAUSE

In order for an abortion to be deemed just, the cause for the abortion must be morally compelling. What this means in a formal sense is that the reasons for seeking the abortion must be such that they justify lifting the moral presumption against abortion. Just abortion will be grounded in the fact that the pregnancy has generated a conflict between the good of life, which the pregnancy is promoting, and other desired goods, which the pregnancy, because of circumstance, is discouraging or preventing from being satisfied. For the pregnant woman who experiences this conflict, those other goods that are in conflict with the good of pregnancy may include such things as the woman's life; her personal and moral integrity; her health and sense of well-being; her ability to function ably as a responsible provider and nurturer; and her capacity to envision a meaningful life and future where she will be able to experience pleasure and enjoyment in work, play, and in her social and familial relationships. In order to consider the abortion option, it must be determined that morally serious reasons related to these other goods of life are forcing a value conflict with the good of life ingredient in the pregnancy. Moreover, those reasons must be so formulated that in a particular circumstance they provide just cause for lifting or overriding the moral presumption against abortion.

Establishing morally serious reasons for justifying abortion does not depend upon identifying some singular reason that by definition will always and universally lead a woman to consider abortion. Morally serious reasons for considering abortion must arise from a consideration of the particularities of a pregnant woman's situation. In just abortion, the pregnancy always provokes a conflict between goods of life. That conflict provides the occasion necessary for articulating a reasoned moral appeal to the possibility of abortion.

There are reasons for desiring an abortion that are insufficient to justify making such a reasoned moral appeal. In her well-known article "A Defense of Abortion," philosopher Judith Jarvis Thomson, who defended a woman's right to decide what she will do with her body, mentions such a case—the woman who is in her seventh month of pregnancy and wants an abortion "just to avoid the nuisance of postponing a trip abroad."[8] Desiring an abortion because of the restrictions pregnancy inevitably places on normal physical activity, or because of simple inconvenience having to do with cosmetic self-image or the altering of lifestyle preferences, would, all things being equal, be insufficient to establish just cause for abortion. Again, just cause emerges from a conflict involving various goods of life, and to establish successfully a just cause for abortion will require one to show that the good of life ingredient in pregnancy is involved in such serious conflict with other goods of life that killing a developing form of human life becomes a reasonable and morally justifiable option.

It is certainly possible that a pregnancy could interfere with a woman's travel plans, or with a desired cosmetic appearance, or with the fit of her clothes, or even with her desire to continue a habit that she should alter for pregnancy (smoking, drinking alcohol, etc.). But these reasons are not sufficiently strong to justify killing a developing form of human life. They are not grounded in a serious value conflict. They present no challenge to the good of life that the good of life—and the moral presumption against abortion—could not reasonably withstand.

The criticism could be made that the examples just noted, while certainly functional for showing what would constitute a trivial and inadequate cause for abortion, are also unrealistic. The argument could be advanced that since an abortion is not trivial either as a topic for moral reflection or as a medical procedure, it would be hard to imagine a woman deciding for an abortion on, say, cosmetic inconvenience grounds alone.

But other, more realistic examples of insufficiently justified abortion are available. One such example would be that of trying to justify an abortion for reasons of gender preference. Abortions are sometimes performed for the sole reason that the fetus is determined to be of a gender that is not valued by a culture or by a couple in a particular situation. Again, depriving a human fetus of life for this reason seems to devalue the good of life and to honor a morally offensive, sexist attitude that is grounded in cultural bias and inadequately developed value commitments. Gender preference is not a candidate for just cause. It does not generate a value conflict that practical reason recognizes as so grave that abortion presents itself as a rational and morally justifiable response to that conflict. Gender preference as a reason for desiring abortion fails to establish a serious moral appeal to the abortion option. It is, in itself, a highly suspect motive, morally speaking, because of the sexist, exploitative, and unjust attitudes toward gender that it entails, for there are no rational grounds for devaluing persons or even potential persons because of gender. Gender preference would not satisfy the test of just cause, and an abortion performed for this reason would be morally impermissible.

It is also worth commenting on physical or genetic defects as possible candidates for establishing just cause. Medical technology has made it possible to detect physical and genetic anomalies in the developing fetus, which then provokes questions about whether a known defective fetus should be aborted. In general, acquiring information that a developing fetus will be in some way biologically defective is itself insufficient to create a morally compelling conflict of values, although there certainly are some fetal defects so grave that a fully engaged moral consideration of the child's best interests will inevitably raise the abortion option. A diagnosis of anencephaly, one form of which was examined in chapter 3, would certainly present such a case. A fetus known to be afflicted with Down's syndrome, however, is more problematic, and the particulars of the situation again must be considered. Down's syndrome does not necessarily deprive the child afflicted with it of meaningful relational possibilities and the prospect of a meaningful life, so that the defect itself is not sufficient grounds for killing the fetus. But that point must then be weighed against the complication that one defect is usually accompanied by others, which should be taken into consideration when making a reasoned moral appeal to the abortion option and in establishing just cause.

While there are reasons that we must say are insufficient to determine a morally compelling cause for abortion, there also are reasons that do meet this test. A pregnancy that presents serious medical complications that endanger the mother's life and well-being is such a reason. Duty does not require that a mother endanger her own life or well-being to promote the good of life involved in a pregnancy. As a moral agent, a pregnant woman is still required to protect herself from harm and danger and to do so in accordance with the canons of prudential reason and the imperative to treat persons, including oneself, with respect. A fetus need not be considered an "aggressor"—or even "innocent," for that matter—in order for a woman to seek an abortion if her life, health, or well-being are in danger because of a pregnancy.

That a mother has a natural moral right to protect herself if her life is endangered by a pregnancy conforms to moral intuitions and explicitly stated moral justifications shared widely in the moral community. Even many persons who consider themselves pro-life find this a situation where an abortion is morally justifiable, with only moral absolutists holding to the position that the mother has no such right because the fetus is itself the moral equivalent of the pregnant woman so that her life cannot be considered in any way more valuable than that of the fetus. People who hold such an extreme moral view usually do so on religious grounds; that is, their faith commits them to a metaphysics of fetal humanity itself grounded in religious belief.

It is interesting to note, and I offer this as an aside, that those who hold the fetus to be the moral equivalent of the pregnant woman, and who thereby deny her the option of abortion on moral grounds even in the case where her life is in danger, are not actually holding the fetus to be the moral equivalent of the woman. The fetus, rather, is being treated as if it were the mother's moral superior, for the good of fetal life is so construed that its value is thought to be sufficient to deny the mother her basic natural right to self-defense.

Theologies and metaphysical theories that hold to a view that fetal life is innocent, and therefore inviolable, endorse a metaphysical-theological belief that innocence renders the life of the fetus more valuable than that of the pregnant woman, for any endangerment the fetus might present the mother is deemed insufficient to justify the mother's acting in self-defense to preserve her own life by killing the fetus. To hold that a pregnant woman does not have a right to protect herself from a fetus involved in medical complications that may kill her is to invest the fetus with moral standing superior to that of the pregnant woman, which thus renders her a fetus' moral inferior. Although there are no secular grounds for holding such a view, some religious persons and communities endorse this position, in a practical if not theoretical sense. This view, which is also offensive to many religious people and faith communities, is based on a religiously grounded metaphysics of moral personhood. Judged by secular standards and even faith standards in some religious traditions, such a view is based on a dubious metaphysics of moral personhood, so much so that the confused and irrational idea of subordinating the woman to the fetus on the issue of fundamental humanity could reasonably be characterized as fanatical.[9]

A medically complicated pregnancy in which a fetus is threatening the mother's life provides the clearest and most widely accepted example of a just cause for lifting the moral presumption against abortion. Abortions performed for this reason are rare, however; but it is also the case that most women who receive abortions justify them morally on the grounds that the pregnancy is threatening, if not to the pregnant woman's health, then to her well-being. It is on the fuzzy issue of well-being that just cause becomes a complicated issue.

What constitutes well-being is not clear and precisely definable. Content can be given to this concern for the pregnant woman's well-being, however, and we can see how concern for well-being is accommodated even by many persons who consider themselves pro-life. Many people in the moral community who identify themselves as pro-life and anti-abortion would think it reasonable to consider abortion in the case of incest or rape. The reason such a justification is so widely accepted, even among persons on the pro-life side of the issue, is not because the fetus is presenting any necessary threat to the mother's physical health or that the fetus has assumed the status of an attacking aggressor and has thereby lost its status as an innocent. The reason to consider abortion in these cases is because the pregnancy is enmeshed in relational entanglements that are deleterious to the mother's well-being. Even many of those who are opposed to abortion acknowledge that there are "mother's well-being" reasons that should be considered, and that these exceptions are sufficiently weighty to actually establish a just cause.[10]

While rape, incest, and the threat to a mother's life are widely regarded by non-absolutists throughout the moral community as legitimate and morally compelling reasons for considering abortion, it is not often made clear why these causes—and for many, no other causes—are so morally compelling. In the case of pregnancy by means of rape and incest, it is clearly the mother's psychological and relational well-being that determines the compelling moral reason sufficient to lift the moral presumption against abortion.[11]

In arguing for just abortion, the well-being criterion ought not to be associated with particular circumstances, such as rape and incest, if pains are not taken to justify why those circumstances provide serious and compelling moral reasons for overruling the presumption against abortion. This is slippery ground. If the reasons related to mother's well-being hold in these cases and establish just cause for abortion, could not other well-being-related reasons also have weight in other kinds of situations? Once that broader case is made, the possibility presents itself that other specific causes of a morally compelling nature can also be appealed to as just causes for abortion.

I hold that pregnancy in the case of rape or incest does involve considerations that are relevant to establishing just cause for abortion in other, seemingly less grave situations. We can get at these broader considerations by asking, What is the moral issue raised in a pregnancy caused by rape and incest?

Such pregnancies—that they are relatively rare is irrelevant at this point—result from the harming of a woman by violence and coercion and relational impropriety. Persons who commit rape or incest act in such a way that they violate their victim's sense of security and well-being, and, beyond that, violate the person's relational integrity. This violation occurs in the case of rape and incest whether or not a woman becomes pregnant. If pregnancy results, however, this violation of relational integrity is so threatening to the woman's continued well-being that considering abortion is justified as a way of continuing to honor the woman as an autonomous moral person, a member of the moral community who ought to be free of coercion and who should not be forced by the moral community into committing herself to a pregnancy when she became pregnant against her will, without her consent, and in a manner that was disrespectful of her personhood, exploitative, physically endangering, and psychologically harmful.

Rape and incest are extreme but common instances of relational violation, but they are not the only kinds of relational violations that might be appealed to when trying to establish just cause for abortion. Consider, for instance, the woman whose dignity and relational integrity have been assaulted by poverty. The presence of poverty in any society indicates that the social system unjustly restricts access to the opportunities that members of the society desire and require if they are to flourish as persons able to exercise their various capabilities—for work, for experiencing pleasure, for making creative contributions to the common good, for living full lives in which as autonomous persons they are able to make choices about how they shall acquire and promote the various goods of life. Poverty prevents people from exercising these capabilities. Poverty turns people from seeking ways to flourish and forces them to concentrate on survival and acquiring necessities. It reduces the number of opportunities and choices that are practically available, and thus demoralizes and even degrades those caught in its grip.

There are poor women who, because of their economic circumstances, may desire to avoid pregnancy. Yet poverty can so affect a woman that she is prevented from taking sufficient control of her life to avoid unwanted pregnancies, which points to a societal failure to work actively so that all persons can make informed choices about pregnancy and contraception.

Many people view unwanted pregnancies among the community of the poor as the sole responsibility of individual women, a self-deceptive ploy that allows them to shirk corporate responsibility and social accountability. But poverty is a societal creation, and society bears responsibility for creating economic circumstances that restrict choice among the poor and disenfranchise them from participating in the society's decision-making processes. Societies that fail to assume responsibility for providing affordable contraception and opportunities for reproductive education, on the basis of which responsible decisions about sexuality and birth control can be made, contribute to the increase in the numbers of unwanted pregnancies and to the probability that abortion rather than contraception will be seen as the way to deal with unwanted pregnancy. Those who hold poor women responsible for their unwanted pregnancies without taking into account all that societies contribute to creating the conditions where unwanted pregnancies arise miss the forest for the trees—and do so in bad faith. Societies create the conditions that increase the likelihood that those unable to afford contraception will face the practical choice of either abortion or bringing to term an unwanted pregnancy. (Refusing societal aid to fund abortions for these unwanted pregnancies continues the assault on women's dignity, and separates poor women even further from the world where women able to justify abortion can then proceed to get one.) A woman is not being treated as an autonomous moral agent if her economic situation precludes her from receiving a safe and justifiable medical abortion in response to her desire to end an unwanted pregnancy. Forcing a poor woman who can justify an abortion to settle for an unsafe medical procedure or to bear unwanted children, sometimes being induced to do so for baby markets, undermines her moral status as a person and unjustly deprives her of reproductive choices available to more affluent women. The society that restricts a poor woman's ability to make choices to avoid unwanted pregnancies contributes to her ability to establish just cause for abortion; such a woman can claim, as an affluent woman may not be able to, that she did not intend to become pregnant and was prevented from exercising contraception options by economic realities. These facts are relevant to determining just cause, for the woman is positioned to argue that society itself, by its social policy commitments and priorities, has placed her in a position where she is coerced into risking unwanted pregnancy, and that such coercion is an assault on her dignity. Her argument for just cause would then proceed in a formal way much like an argument for justifying abortion in the case of rape or incest—at issue is the violation of relational integrity.

A pregnant woman's relational integrity is rendered vulnerable to violation in an impoverished economic and social experience. A just cause for abortion must never look at a woman's circumstances in isolation from the society of which she is a part, for in the presence of poverty and all that poverty does to limit people's choices and violate their integrity, society, representing the moral community at large, must assume responsibility for helping to create conditions where unwanted pregnancies are not adequately avoided and abortion becomes a means of post-conception birth control.

In establishing just cause for abortion, we must take into consideration the woman's situation and circumstances as well as her desire to terminate her pregnancy because doing so will preserve her well-being and relational integrity. Women who do not want to get pregnant have a responsibility to act so that they avoid pregnancy, and establishing that a woman did not consent to becoming pregnant is certainly relevant to establishing just cause. A failed contraceptive device, for instance, would establish just cause, for the argument could be advanced that by using a device to prevent pregnancy, the woman had acted responsibly with respect to the intention to avoid an unwanted pregnancy. Seeking abortion in this situation would be a way of preventing the woman from being coerced into establishing a moral relation with an unwelcome, intrusive, and unintended relational partner (the fetus). Continuing an unwanted pregnancy in this situation could be said to violate the woman's relational integrity and moral autonomy, and this would also be the case in rape or incest or situations like that of forced marriage.

We cannot focus exclusively on the individual woman's action in relation to her intention to avoid unwanted pregnancy. We must also attend to societal complicity in creating the conditions where abortion becomes an option when those who want to avoid unwanted pregnancies find themselves unable to act consistently with their desires and intentions because of social situation and economic circumstance. In a social situation where society fails to empower women to act so that they might avoid unwanted pregnancies, that failure of social responsibility becomes a critical factor in determining what it means to talk about an assault on a woman's well-being and a violation of her relational integrity; and this social factor then must be allowed to play a role in determining just cause. In the light of the high teenage pregnancy rate, it could also be said that young women who would certainly not want to get pregnant but who do, having failed to receive an education in sexuality and reproduction, and whose ignorance has not been corrected by a society determined to help empower even teenaged women to know what they are doing when they fail to act to prevent unwanted pregnancy, are positioned to launch a similar claim for just cause if the society fails to assist and empower them to make responsible choices.

The woman who would, in my interpretation, have the most difficulty establishing just cause for abortion would be a woman of relative affluence who, with her sexual partner, is able to acquire contraception without undo economic hardship; who has available educational resources so that it can be said with some assurance that she understands what is involved in human sexuality and reproduction and family responsibilities; who consented to the sexual act that led to conception; who chose with her partner not to use a contraceptive device, when doing so would have imposed no hardship; and whose capacities for making decisions about contraception were not impaired. If these conditions are met, just cause would be difficult to establish without some other factor coming into play. The couple has acted in such a way that it seems reasonable to say that they did, in fact, intend a pregnancy, and the moral rationale for aborting the fetus involved in this situation would have to come from other factors, such as a medical complication.

Just cause will concern itself with such traditional matters as whether individuals seeking to avoid a pregnancy act consistently with that intention. Should that be demonstrated, it would be coercive to force a woman or couple who acted to prevent a pregnancy from proceeding with it, for doing so violates the relational integrity of persons. Just cause will attend to medical condition and to the best interests of the prospective child—there are some biological anomalies so severe that aborting the fetus would serve the best interests not only of the mother (and father) and even society, but the prospective newborn itself. This kind of child-centered focus, as reflected in the just non-treatment of severely handicapped newborns discussed in the previous chapter, is certainly relevant to our consideration of just cause for abortion. And just cause will attend to the well-being of the mother, not just individually in a physical and psychological sense, but in a corporate dimension, too. For a woman caught in the grip of an unwanted pregnancy cannot be held accountable for that pregnancy as if the society of which she is a part is not in some way contributing to the situation that prevents women like her, who want to avoid pregnancy, from actually doing so. By failing to provide such things as sex education and affordable and available contraception, societal priorities, as manifested in the channeling of economic and educational resources, can be such that they reveal a society not committed to helping persons act consistently with their desire to avoid unwanted pregnancy. Society itself becomes a responsible agent that must be held accountable for creating conditions that can be appealed to as just cause for abortion. Societies make decisions and expend resources that contribute to the increase in the number of unwanted abortions; for society then to coerce women into bringing to term their unwanted pregnancies would constitute action that would violate the relational integrity of human persons. It would do harm to the well-being of women, demean them, and deprive them of their status of autonomous

moral persons. Making the abortion option available and allowing women to exercise that option would prevent such gross
moral impropriety from occurring. And even though the abortion option will involve the killing of a developing form of human life, that killing, as we see most clearly when a pregnancy
is threatening to a woman's life or has come about through rape
or incest, is not so grave as the moral offense that would occur
were an unwanted pregnancy to continue under coercion and by
means that violate women's relational integrity. That would visit
harm on the pregnant woman and possibly even the future neonate, with whom the mother would establish moral relationship. Determining just cause for abortion will require that this
kind of analysis be presented so that the moral presumption
against abortion can be justifiably overruled in a particular instance of unwanted pregnancy.

## CRITERION 3: LAST RESORT

In order for an abortion to be considered just, all other options
for dealing with the fact of an unwanted pregnancy must be
considered prior to electing the abortion option. Abortion ought
to be treated as a last resort. Why it ought to be so regarded
depends upon a point already made: abortion involves the killing
of a developing form of human life; and because that life is
interpreted as deserving of the protection afforded by a moral
presumption against abortion, killing it requires justification.

One need not embrace the view that a young fetus is a person
to hold that as a developing form of human life, it possesses at
least an incipient moral status. It is that status, based on the
good of life ingredient in the pregnancy itself, that is recognized
in the moral presumption against abortion. Whatever else that
moral presumption against abortion might mean, it at least
means that a fetus, even a young fetus, ought not to be killed
casually or unreflectively or without good and morally compelling reason. The moral presumption against abortion would require that women faced with unwanted pregnancy consider and
deliberate on all possible options, not just the abortion option.
Electing the abortion option ought to be the result of determin-

ing that the value conflicts involved cannot be satisfactorily settled by employing other available options.[12]

A just abortion will require, then, that as a function of last resort the options of bringing an unwanted fetus to term and raising it as one's own, giving it up for adoption, or contracting with a childless couple be considered and evaluated. If there is a way to resolve the value conflicts involved in an unwanted pregnancy short of choosing abortion, it would be morally incumbent upon persons to consider doing so. As a practical matter, this criterion is considered prior to almost any abortion, for the criterion simply means that a woman faced with an unwanted pregnancy would, if given a reasonable alternative to abortion, select that alternative before seeking an abortion. It could be said that every time a couple uses birth control to avoid an unwanted pregnancy, they invoke this criterion implicitly. By using contraceptives, a couple would be acting consistently with their desire to avoid abortion as a possible solution to unwanted pregnancy. Using contraceptive devices is a practical and morally uncomplicated way to endorse the view that abortion ought to be a last resort in dealing with an unwanted pregnancy, for it is morally preferable to act to prevent an unwanted pregnancy than to risk placing oneself in a position where abortion might become a live option.

The criticism could be made that to talk about contraceptive use is unresponsive to the context where the last resort criterion applies. For the last resort criterion really concerns only a woman who is already pregnant and who is facing an either/or decision: either bring the already alive fetus to term or abort it. However, we must consider another argument that naturally follows from the idea that abortion ought to be a last resort.

Last resort would seem to throw weight in the direction of bringing the fetus to term, for the good of life ingredient in fetal life ought to outweigh most considerations that would lead to the irrevocable option of killing. In other words, if one is given the option of allowing a fetus to live or killing it, observing last resort would necessarily tip the balance in favor of life against death, for life is a good of life and a moral presumption promoting and protecting that life attached to it. By saying that abortion is a last resort, one is saying that this killing ought to be avoided if it can be avoided, and that prima facie one ought not to kill the fetus because doing so is a final and irrevocable move. If abortion is really a last resort, the prospect of bringing an unwanted fetus to term seems the lesser of two evils and, at least compared to death, not so grave an inconvenience for the mother. Last resort, it could be argued, would pit a morally problematic solution to unwanted pregnancy, abortion, against a relatively unproblematic solution, namely, bringing a fetus to term. In that conflict between options, observing last resort would justify only those abortions where a woman's life is in danger or where the abortion could be argued as being in the interests of the prospective baby. Otherwise, last resort would commend bringing the fetus to term and avoiding the abortion option.

There are two assumptions in the above argument that must not go unchallenged. The first is that the life of the fetus is clearly a good that outweighs the other goods that the pregnant woman finds conflicting with the good of fetal life and that have contributed to her determination that the pregnancy is unwanted. To assert that last resort necessitates honoring fetal life as if it were not enmeshed in problematic relations with these other goods is to move in the direction of absolutizing the good of fetal life. If this is accomplished, then the prospective mother is being asked to bow to the good of fetal life and deny that she is in any position to act as a moral agent able to make difficult but morally justifiable decisions with respect to preserving her relational integrity vis-à-vis an unwanted pregnancy. For a pregnant woman not to consider abortion because the last resort criterion necessitates that if she is able to bring an unwanted pregnancy to term she must do so—the one obvious exception being to protect her own life from a medically endangering pregnancy—is to present a conflict with our first criterion of just abortion. The assumption that abortion must be a last resort in the sense that any possible way of preserving fetal life is preferable to killing a fetus actually positions the mother as a moral inferior to the fetus. This is, as previously argued, a morally reprehensible and unjustifiable move to make.

The other assumption involved in the above argument is that

the option of bringing a fetus to term is either not problematic or clearly not so problematic as abortion. This is to deny the reality of the moral conflict that has given rise to the pregnancy being unwanted in the first place. It cannot simply be assumed that the available options one confronts when facing an unwanted pregnancy are a morally problematic solution (abortion) versus one that is clearly not morally problematic (bringing the pregnancy to term). Were this a fair characterization of the value conflict at stake, one would also have to assume that bringing an unwanted pregnancy to term is always in the best interests of the child and mother, that allowing an unwanted child to be raised by persons who do not want it provokes no serious moral issues, and that the adoption option is itself not morally problematic.

These beliefs do not withstand critical scrutiny. Allowing an unwanted pregnancy to come to term does not allow one to escape moral problems and value conflicts. A woman who is denied the option of abortion and is forced to establish an unwanted maternal relationship and bring an unwanted pregnancy to term has not thereby eliminated moral problems and value conflicts. Those conflicts have been relocated and made even more complex, for the mother who brings an unwanted pregnancy to term against her will does so under some kind of coercion that subverts her relational integrity and that of the mother-child relationship. Giving a child up for adoption—a topic that needs more ethical evaluation than I can give at present—seems at least to raise serious moral questions, for the mother is being forced into a promise-keeping relation with a developing fetus. That moral relation between mother and child is broken once the baby is born and given up for adoption, so that the relational integrity of mother and child is broken, and that break is not without moral interest. This act of giving up is not non-problematic from a moral point of view, especially if the mother is continuing with the pregnancy for money (surrogacy) or because she is under coercion of some sort, which is again indicative of moral violation. This should not be interpreted as a moral condemnation of those who give up children for adoption, but only as an indication that choosing adoption over abortion does not necessarily eliminate moral problems or construe the options as a morally problematic one (abortion) versus a non-problematic one (adoption).

The options of bringing a child to term and either keeping it as an unwanted child or giving it up for adoption are not without moral problems of their own. These options ought to be considered prior to electing abortion. But the good of life, while preeminent, is not absolute, and the circumstances at issue in particular pregnancies may help women and couples decide that the option of bringing a baby to term not only does not resolve the value conflict raised by the unwanted pregnancy, but makes it worse, in which case abortion, even as a last resort, may justifiably become the option of choice.

## CRITERION 4. MEDICAL SUCCESS

An abortion that endangers a mother's life ought not to be performed. In order for an abortion to be justified, one must have reason to believe that the pregnant woman will not face a more substantial risk of harm by going through the medical procedure of abortion than by going through a pregnancy. Since there is a time in fetal gestation where the medical risk of abortion is about the same as that associated with continued pregnancy,[13] this criterion would restrict abortions to the time where abortion is itself medically safer to the pregnant woman than continued pregnancy.

The function of this criterion is to ensure that a justifiable abortion can be performed safely. Invoking this criterion helps argue for the point that it is more difficult morally to justify an abortion the longer the pregnancy proceeds, not simply because the fetus grows and matures and all that that entails for moral consideration (see criterion 6 in chapter 5), but because the risk of medical complication for the mother necessarily increases. This criterion argues that should the risk increase to the point that the abortion is more dangerous to the health and well-being of the mother than the pregnancy, the pregnancy should not be terminated.

Very simply, a woman who has good and morally justifiable reasons for electing abortion should be assured that the medical procedure involved in abortion is itself safe and does not pose a greater risk to her health and welfare than continued pregnancy. Practically speaking, this means that she ought to be fully informed about the procedure and assured that competent medical personnel will perform it; that any medical complications will receive follow-up treatment; and that she and her medical care providers will be secure in their persons in facilities where abortions are performed.

When a pregnancy reaches that stage where on medical grounds continuing it is safer than terminating it, abortion ought not to be chosen; and choosing abortion does not allow for the killing of a fetus that, upon removal, is medically determined to be viable. For an abortion to be considered a just abortion, this "medical success" criterion must be satisfied, along with the other five.

## CRITERION 5: PRESERVING VALUES/NON-SUBVERSION OF THE VALUE OF LIFE

When a pregnancy is determined to be unwanted, a value conflict is created. At stake in the conflict are goods that the pregnancy promotes, especially the good of life and the good of participating in family life, and goods that a continued pregnancy will prevent from being realized. These other goods could include such things as the mother's life and well-being, the well-being and best interests of the prospective child, the preservation of the mother's relational integrity and moral status vis-à-vis the fetus, and whatever other goods that are so challenging the good of life ingredient in the pregnancy that the woman is led to interpret the pregnancy as undesirable and unwanted. Abortion presents one possible way that the value conflict at stake in an unwanted pregnancy can be resolved. This fifth criterion of just abortion requires that if this option is elected, then the loss of the good of life involved in the killing of the fetus will be done to preserve important values, such as the woman's life or well-being, or the mother's relational integrity or her moral status vis-à-vis the fetus. In harmony with the test of just cause and last resort, a just abortion will also be required, under this criterion, to preserve important values that could not otherwise be preserved, and to do so while being non-subversive to the value of life itself.

In the just abortion theory being proposed here, abortion is never reducible to a medical procedure—it is always a moral problem that has at its heart a conflict of value and moral meaning. This preservation of value criterion reinforces the idea that solving the value conflict generated by an unwanted pregnancy can never be a casual or morally trivial decision. Just abortion requires that the person seeking the abortion do so with the intention of preserving important values that otherwise cannot be preserved. We have seen, in our discussion of just cause, how this may happen when what is at stake is the mother's life or well-being, her moral status vis-à-vis the fetus, or even the prospective well-being of the fetus itself. The particularities of the value conflict will differ according to the particularities of the unwanted pregnancy, but the general point this criterion of just abortion makes is that the conflict must be present, that it must be recognizable as a serious conflict, and that to satisfy this criterion is to determine that the conflict is so serious that the good of life may be justifiably sacrificed to other goods that could not be preserved were the pregnancy to continue. A mother who aborts a fetus seeking to preserve the good of her own life, which may include her physical well-being or her relational integrity, is positioned to satisfy this criterion.

But the criterion addresses another issue as well. For in addition to requiring that an abortion preserve values that could not otherwise be preserved, it also requires that one do no harm to, or in any way subvert, the value of the good of life that is protected by the moral presumption against abortion. In other words, the moral presumption against abortion that was lifted in the particular situation so that a morally justifiable abortion could be performed must be reinstated. Even after an abortion, the value of the good of life ingredient in pregnancy must continue to be recognized as a good of life; it must not be attenuated by the abortion, and the moral presumption against abortion must not be obscured.

This criterion of just abortion, along with last resort and just cause, supports the general idea that abortion ought not to become a means or method of birth control. Because abortion is a killing and requires moral justification, preventing the situation that gives rise to unwanted pregnancy is always the preferable course. Contraception as a way of preventing unwanted pregnancy is always preferable to facing an actual situation of unwanted pregnancy where bearing an unwanted child or killing the fetus are the only options for ending the pregnancy. Both of these options are morally problematic. If abortion rather than contraception becomes a preferred means of ending unwanted pregnancies, the moral presumption against abortion may itself be weakened, and that could indicate that the good of life itself, even such life as a developing fetus possesses, is being devalued and trivialized. Just abortion seeks in particular situations and circumstances to lift the moral presumption against abortion, not subvert it. Once an abortion is performed, it seeks to restore that presumption intact, not in weakened form.

Moral consequentialists often argue against abortion on the grounds that the availability of abortions increases their frequency, and in a society where abortions continue to increase, this frequency may have a deleterious impact on how the value of life is regarded. While I take this point seriously, I do not, as an advocate of the just abortion approach, want to concede it. Just abortion will ask that we not confuse the issue of a morally justifiable abortion with the number of abortions that might be performed in a particular society, any of which may be just or unjust.

In the former Soviet Union, abortion did become a method of birth control. The Soviet Union had the highest rate of abortion in the world, with the average Soviet woman terminating between five and seven pregnancies during her reproductive years.[14] Not only were abortions frequent among individual women, but the society as a whole had a high percentage of abortions to pregnancies carried to term. However, I have seen no evidence that the women who received sometimes shockingly high numbers of abortions in their childbearing years came to devalue the good of life ingredient in pregnancy. Anecdotal evidence would suggest just the opposite: there are reports of Soviet women who had double-digit abortions in their childbearing years and who felt grieved and dispirited—even de-graded—by having to opt for abortion so often. Here is where we must draw an important distinction. Responsibility for a society's reliance on abortion to end unwanted pregnancy should not rest on the individual's shoulders if the society itself has made reducing the number of abortions practically impossible. In the case of the Soviet Union, the society did not reevaluate its priorities and invest resources into making affordable birth control available to those who wanted it. The society must be held accountable for any diminishing of the value of life that could be said to have resulted from a high number of abortions.

Just abortion is a theory of moral responsibility that involves not only individual women (and men) who are faced with un-wanted pregnancies, but the societies and economic systems that either seek to help persons avoid unwanted pregnancies or pre-vent them from doing so. Societies that place the entire moral burden for unwanted pregnancy on the individual woman, that fail to provide education and make affordable contraception available, create an environment where abortions will tend to become more frequent rather than less so. This social environ-ment can restrict what choices persons have with respect to avoiding unwanted pregnancy and coerce them into risking un-wanted pregnancy when their preference clearly would be oth-erwise. In such a social system, women who are forced to opt for abortion rather than share responsibility for contraception are being treated disrespectfully, as if facing the abortion option were not a serious and morally troubling prospect. The value of life is degraded when a society makes it easier to kill live fe-tuses—while subjecting women to an invasive and always po-tentially risky medical procedure—than to offer the safer, less risky, and less morally problematic alternative of contraception. I cannot say whether—or how—life becomes devalued as the result of individual abortions, but such devaluation would seem to accompany social policy priorities in which the numbers of abortion increase as abortion becomes a primary form of birth control.

A just abortion must be one that does not express a cheapen-ing of the value of life. A just abortion lifts the moral presumption against abortion but then restores it so that it in no way subverts commitment to honoring the value of life. In societies like that of the former Soviet Union and even our own, a high number of abortions may very well represent a social, economic, and political commitment to policies and priorities that do subvert the value of life, and high numbers of abortion can be seen as one indication of a broader life-subverting tendency. The solution to the moral problem created when a society establishes priorities and pursues policies that degrade the value of life is not to prevent individual women from obtaining justifiable abortions, but for the society to accept responsibility for its role in creating the conditions that increase the likelihood that abortion will be a means of birth control. This is a social justice question of tremendous moral importance. And while the number of abortions in any given society may have relevance to just abortion— especially since those numbers may factor into establishing just cause—the numbers themselves are not the direct focus. Just abortion attends always to the particularities of a situation in the light of a moral presumption against abortion.

The moral meaning of all that a society does to increase the likelihood of abortion and to contribute to the rise in the number of abortions must be considered and evaluated as a moral issue on its own, separate from applying just abortion criteria to a particular abortion. Women, even those who have had multiple abortions, can meet the preserving values/non-subversion of life criterion in their individual situations even if they live in a society where abortions have come to serve as a primary means of birth control. The fact that a society might be pursuing policies and priorities that, say, limit the availability of affordable birth control could be used, ironically, to help establish just cause and last resort, for societal complicity in creating situations that promote unwanted pregnancies becomes a factor as individual women evaluate their situation to determine whether a pregnancy is unwanted.

In a society where people facing unwanted pregnancy are forced to the abortion option, the society itself must bear responsibility for creating social and economic conditions that subvert the value of life of particular people or groups of people.

This moral responsibility applies even if many in the society would deny it, even if many in the society would support policies to restrict and even to outlaw abortions in the name of pro-life. If action is not also taken to address the corporate dimension of the problem, then advocating pro-life social policies without attending to all that societies do to contribute to the increase in the number of abortions becomes a self-contradictory move. Pro-life policies that emphasize individual responsibility while minimizing societal responsibility are self-deceptive, for at the same time that they affirm life and oppose abortion, they deny all that the society does to promote abortion as a solution to unwanted pregnancy and all that the society does to create conditions that degrade the value of life. One should not conclude from this that social policy determines the moral permissibility of abortion in individual cases. Individual cases provide the appropriate arena for deciding just abortion. The fact that a society may subvert the value of life by its policies and priorities does not mean that women who are living in that society and facing the abortion option cannot, because of their societal context, satisfy the preserving values/non-subversion of life criterion.

# 5

# The Theory of
# Just Abortion II

I now address the most difficult abortion problem—fetal human-ity. At stake is the question, How are we to evaluate the moral meaning of the biological facts involved in fetal development? This question is important because the pro-life and pro-choice sides of the abortion debate have evaluated the moral meaning of the biological facts differently, and opposing absolutists on the question of moral meaning have excluded a priori the possibility of agreement on this issue.

I shall point out possible ways to construct a rational disagree-ment from a common point of moral reference, the moral pre-sumption against abortion. There is a rational foundation for holding in a non-absolutist way the position that a fetus is a person—a member of the moral community—from conception. By virtue of refusing to hold this as an absolutist view, we open the door to possible exceptions to the moral presumption against abortion, and to the possibility of a just abortion. On the pro-choice side, recognition of the moral presumption against abor-tion will determine that there is a point when the developing form of human life at issue in pregnancy is and ought to be granted admission into the moral community, so that its life is thereby entitled to protection. The possibility of abortion is thereby practically excluded, although, since this exclusion does not issue from an absolutist position, exceptions are certainly possible.

Articulating these non-absolutist views around the question of fetal humanity will expose the common ground that the moral presumption against abortion creates for those who defend different views of fetal humanity.

Rather than looking at the biological facts of fetal development and concluding from those facts that a fetus either is or is not a person, as if the facts themselves could settle such a dispute, I shall use those facts to inform a *moral* discussion about the *moral* meaning of fetal humanity and the *moral* problem provoked by the abortion issue. I shall argue that the moral institution of promise-keeping is the critical moral pivot on which disagreement over the question of fetal humanity should turn. I, too, shall appeal to biological data to support a particular argument about fetal humanity, but my argument will seek to use those data as a way of supporting a moral criterion that must be in place for an abortion to be considered just. It is to this moral criterion and its relevance to just abortion theory that I now turn.

## CRITERION 6. PRIOR-TO-PROMISE

At what point is one entitled to treat a fetus as if it were a person so that it can be extended membership in the moral community and receive protection from that community? Is there some cut-off point in fetal development at which one can say that abortions before this point are permitted and beyond it they are not? And is that point determined on scientific grounds, moral grounds, some combination, or is it, rather, arbitrary?

There are no questions more difficult in the abortion issue than these. Yet just abortion theory does provide a guideline for determining some point in a pregnancy when an abortion is eligible for moral justification and beyond which it is not. The approach of just abortion is not concerned primarily with the intrinsic developmental status of the fetus, for appealing to certain facts about biological development does not answer the moral question but rather begs it. If we consider the facts of fetal development, this becomes clearer. Following is a list of the developmental stages through which a fetus passes on the way to live birth:

1. *Conception* occurs twenty-four hours after a sperm penetrates the ovum. The forty-six chromosomes are arranged as a complete set of human genes, making the conceptus a member of the human species.
2. *Implantation*, when the fertilized egg attaches to the uterine wall, occurs six to seven days after conception.
3. *Individuation* identifies the fourteen-day period after conception when twinning and mosaic recombination are possible.
4. *The heart starts beating* three to four weeks after conception.
5. *All organs are present* in rudimentary stage by week six, and the fetus begins to look human.
6. A *reflex response* to pain and tickling stimuli is present: week seven.
7. *Brain waves*, emanating from the brain stem, are detectable: week eight.
8. *Spontaneous movement* independent of stimulation begins: week ten.
9. The *brain* can be said to have a complete structure: week twelve.
10. *Quickening*, which is the moment a pregnant woman feels the fetus move, occurs between twelve and sixteen weeks.
11. A *10 percent probability of survival* outside the womb is established by twenty weeks.
12. *Viability* outside the womb occurs as the lungs and other organs are sufficiently developed to support independent life: twenty-four to twenty-eight weeks.
13. *Conscious awareness* can be inferred from the appearance of distinct sleep versus brain wave patterns: twenty-eight weeks.

14. *The eyes* reopen after being shut since week thirteen: twenty-eight to thirty weeks.
15. *Normal birth*: forty weeks.
16. *Self-consciousness, language use, and rationality* begin one to two years after birth.[1]

These facts about fetal development beg the question about fetal humanity for the following reason: nothing in any of the facts pertaining to fetal development determines uncontroversially the moral standing of the fetus. Nothing that can be extracted from the data of development determines as a factual matter that personhood ought to be attributed, conferred, or recognized at one moment rather than at another. Personhood, remember, is a moral category, and these empirical facts about biological development, while they may be used to develop or support moral theories or positions on fetal humanity, are simply facts that await moral interpretation. Such developmental data are not morally self-explanatory—the moral meaning of any particular biological fact is simply not self-evident. The interpretive chore is to establish the relevance of certain facts to any particular theory one might wish to advance.

If there is a descriptive or sociological fact about fetal development that can be taken into account without controversy it is this: different moral communities appeal to different metaphysical theories to establish personhood at particular points in this developmental process. The Roman Catholic church, for instance, recognizes personhood and commends fetal protection from the moment of conception. Others, like psychiatrist Thomas Szasz, take a radically different view and hold that a conceptus is a meaningless lump of tissue.[2] Again, how one determines this issue directly affects one's view concerning the moral permissibility of abortion. Whereas the Roman Catholic position on fetal humanity would prohibit abortion as a direct attack on the good of life and as an unjustified killing of an innocent human person, the Szasz view would render an abortion of an unwanted fetus the moral equivalent of a tooth extraction.

Both the Roman Catholic and the Szasz view look to the reality of biological development to draw moral conclusions about moral status. Just abortion theory, however, does not look to biological development, at least in the first instance, to determine the point at which the moral determination about personhood is to be made. Rather, it recognizes personhood as a moral category, so that just abortion is concerned first and foremost with the moral idea of being in relation.

If we focus on biological development, rather than on the moral relation a pregnant woman enters into with her fetus, inevitable problems arise. Any biological fact that one may wish to use for moral determinations about personhood must be shown to be relevant to the moral enterprise of determining the meaning and moment of personhood. This is obviously difficult to do; it is so difficult that we as a society have failed to achieve anything approaching moral consensus on this point. Looking to biological facts about fetal development will not yield a clear and decisive moral interpretation that will settle our societal division about abortion. Abortion is a moral problem, a problem over moral interpretation. It is not a dispute about biological facts as facts, but about what the facts mean.

Let us consider some questions and arguments. Could we seriously entertain the possibility of marking the moment of personhood at that point two years after birth when the young child is able to actually exercise reason and speech and whatever criteria we ascribe to those who hold the office of person? To do that would open us to the possibility of justifying morally the practice of infanticide, since an infant less than two years old would not be admitted into the moral community. Even considering this possibility is morally repugnant. Clearly personhood can be—and is—ascribed by the moral community prior to seeing evidence that a particular human being has so developed that it can exercise whatever capacities we wish to ascribe to persons.

But does the moral community recognize personhood at the point of viability, or is it only appropriate to extend it at the moment of birth? And then, what is morally relevant developmentally about a fetus two days prior to a term delivery versus a live birth baby? Biological development is not what determines the moral question about personhood. Let us consider another, more widely accepted argument that locates personhood at a particular developmental point, and show how we run into problems even there.

What if we were to advance the argument that the moral community should establish personhood at the moment the fetus is able to feel pain? The question this poses is obvious: Why is the capacity to feel pain sufficient to establish personhood, when the fetus that would feel pain lacks the self-consciousness to interpret that pain as its own? Would we not then be committed to the view that we should admit into the moral community any sentient creature capable of feeling pain? If the biological capacity to feel pain (not interpret it) is to be the distinguishing characteristic of personhood, then it could be argued that we should have to admit all kinds of sentient but non-human creatures into the moral community since non-human animals also feel pain. And if the retort came back that we must restrict our moral community to human animals, then we face the problem that something other than the capacity to feel pain is what distinguishes human animals as members of the moral community from non-members. That distinguishing characteristic would have to be something such as species membership; and species membership is biologically determined at conception, not at the point where a fetus is capable of feeling pain.

We could argue for other points in fetal development as well, but no point is free from problems. There are even interesting metaphysical and religious problems that arise. One could argue, internal to the Roman Catholic metaphysical view of person-from-conception, that the theological reason for recognizing personhood at conception is that the conceptus is endued with the good of life, that the good of life is a gift of God, that the conceptus is created in God's image, and that it possesses, even in its earliest moments of life, an immortal soul.[3] Souls are by definition indivisible. A metaphysical problem arises when one considers that up to fourteen days after fertilization, an egg can split. When this occurs, identical twins are formed. If the fertilized egg is possessed of a soul, then splits into identical twins, where is the soul? Does it go into one of the fertilized eggs and not the other, so that one of the twins is soulless; or does it split so that each has half a soul? Couple this with the fact that occasionally two fertilized eggs will combine to form one egg at the point of individuation. Does this being now possess two souls, since the soul of each of the individual eggs that combined in the mosaic, as this phenomenon is called by biologists, must still be present?[4] Holding to the person-from-conception view because of a metaphysics related to the possession of the soul at the moment of conception introduces problems. And those problems are created because of what we know about certain peculiar biological processes.

We are in the arena of differing religious views—a point that ought not to be taken lightly in discussions of abortion, for it is differing religious views that are at stake in the fetal humanity question, at least until that point in fetal development where we can come together as a moral community and agree that *at this point* we can confer membership in the moral community on the fetus. But even religious arguments that try to establish a metaphysical basis for recognizing personhood at a particular point in fetal development (i.e., conception) can run aground because of metaphysical inconsistencies or absurd implications.

I have pointed to a religious reason for holding to the view that a fetus is a person from the moment of conception. I have shown one way of construing it so that it appears fraught with rational inconsistencies even on the religious premise that a fertilized egg is God's creature and possessed of an immortal soul. Although one might simply reject such religious metaphysical conceptions of person out of hand, the more serious question in secular society might be this: Are there rational grounds for acknowledging personhood from the moment of conception?

A positive case can be made that there are rational grounds for holding to the person-from-conception perspective. I do not ultimately find this rational argument compelling since I hold to a relational argument, which does not depend in the first instance upon biological development concerns. The rational argument for person-from-conception, as opposed to the faith-related view of souls as present in fertilized eggs, would go like this: Since imputing the moral category of person to a member of the human species cannot be determined by any clear and inarguable facts that pertain to a particular point in fetal development, we ought, as a matter of erring on the side of the good of life that even a fertilized egg possesses, treat even the conceptus as if it were a person, giving it the benefit of the doubt. In other words, we should impute personhood to the member of the human species at its earliest moment of being identifiable as a member of the species, not by faith or dogma, but out of *moral skepticism*: since I cannot know for a fact when a fetus becomes a person, but I do know it is alive and that life is a good of life, I must grant it protection from the earliest moment possible for the very reason that I cannot know. I must give the fetus the benefit of the doubt and extend protection to it from the moment of conception, and I do this knowing that all living persons must have a beginning in their biological lives, and that this biological beginning is a necessary condition in all that happens to members of the human species as they develop into members of the moral community and are recognized as persons.

This rational argument for person-from-conception is distinct from that advanced by those in Christian faith traditions, Protestant or Roman Catholic, who look to dogma or Scripture to determine the moral meaning of fetal humanity. Those who so interpret the tradition as to oppose all abortions on the grounds that abortion unjustly kills a person—a child of God—express a viewpoint on person-from-conception that is morally absolutist. The rational argument, however, being based not on dogma but on doubt and on the granting of the benefit of the doubt earlier in development rather than later, is not absolutist. In fact, this rational person-from-conception view is not incompatible with just abortion, for the basis for holding this view is moral skepticism—a confession of not knowing—and not knowing precludes dogmatic claims to certainty. The skepticism that commits us to the view that we cannot achieve certainty about when in fetal development personhood begins, also commits us to a non-absolutist position when extending the benefit of the doubt. To hold the person-from-conception view on rational grounds in the face of not knowing for certain is to hold open the possibility that one could lift the protections one extends to persons in the face of compelling reasons for doing so and in light of the fact that we cannot know for certain. Another way to construct this position is to say that there is a rational defense for holding to the person-from-conception view, but that this rational argument, because it is constructed in the face of not knowing when personhood obtains, simply states a hard case for the moral presumption against abortion. Because this rational position is not—and cannot be—committed to a morally absolutist position, it also refuses to appeal to any grounds—rational or dogmatic—that would absolutely prohibit one from lifting that presumption in compelling cases or circumstances.

If just abortion evades the moral interpretation of biological criteria—at least as a formal response to the question of when a fetus becomes a person—then we are entitled to ask, on what basis does just abortion extend protection to the fetus—if at all? Does just abortion recognize some point in fetal development beyond which abortions ought not be permitted? If so, what is it, and why is that point rather than another selected?

Just abortion, because it treats the issue of abortion as a moral problem, seeks to establish a criterion that addresses the question of fetal humanity. Because there is a moral presumption against abortion, the fetus cannot be treated as if it were of no moral significance at all. On the other hand, the developmental facts are arguable with respect to fetal humanity, so that there is no absolutely certain point before birth at which the facts of fetal development compel all rational persons to accept that at this point and no other the fetus actually becomes, for this reason or that, a person, and is thus entitled to be protected from abortion.

The approach just abortion theory takes at this point is to consider moral relations and the inescapable fact that the moral community does have a vital interest in the fetus' life that the fetus cannot express for itself. That interest in fetal life is articulated by the moral community as a moral presumption against abortion. To the extent that the Thomas Szasz position seems not to acknowledge this moral presumption against abortion, it must be rejected as failing to acknowledge life, even fetal life, as a foundational good of life that deserves to be promoted and protected.

I advocate shifting attention away from the complex of metaphysical entanglements that focus on the fetus as a developing form of human life that actually or potentially possesses certain properties we ascribe (or not) to persons. This has been a typical topic of discussion in most philosophical and even religious discussions of abortion—even I cannot avoid it, as I shall point out. But approaching the abortion issue by examining the fetus for properties of personhood, either metaphysical or biological, simply raises more issues than it settles; and, again, no consensus has been achieved as to what are the critical, necessary, and sufficient conditions for ascribing personhood.

Jane English was one of the first to indicate that there are no easy demarcation points for locating personhood in fetal development, and no single criterion to which we can appeal in order to claim that one fetus is a person and another is not.[5] The kind of epistemological and moral skepticism embodied in her view is appropriate to the issue because the moral question of personhood cannot be settled by an appeal to facts about fetal development. What is needed is a moral argument about fetal humanity that addresses the moral relations at stake in the abortion question, so that the abortion option is not misconstrued as simply a medical response to a biological condition (pregnancy). To preserve abortion as a moral problem, we must remain focused on moral issues and not stray into debates about biological development as if they were the primary concern, for such discussions often proceed on the assumption that the moral meaning of biological data is inarguably clear, uncontroversial, or even self-evident.

I propose to keep this focus on the moral relations involved in abortion by shifting attention away from biological development to the moral relation that obtains between the pregnant woman and the fetus she is carrying. Now the question becomes not when is the fetus a person, but at what point is fetal life protected because the fetus has received a promise of life, a promise from the pregnant woman—either explicitly or implicitly—that it shall be brought to term? At what point in a pregnancy does a mother (or the moral community) determine that her fetus is wanted and on the basis of that determination enter into a moral relation with the fetus that entails a promise to bring it to term? This represents a shifting of the moral issue away from properties of personhood and the facts of biological development to the fact that pregnancy involves a moral relation based on a promise made to the fetus. As promise-keeping is foundational in all moral relations, and it is morally impermissible to break promises in our moral relations, it follows that an abortion is morally impermissible once a mother has promised to bring a fetus to term.[6]

When in pregnancy is this moral relation between mother and fetus established? There is no single point that covers all instances. A woman who wants to get pregnant and wants to bring a fetus to term may enter into a moral, promise-keeping relation with her fetus as soon as she knows she is pregnant. From that earliest moment she will regard the fetus as if it were a person, not because of any inherent properties that the conceptus might possess as a biological entity, but because the woman has, even at that early point in pregnancy, affirmed the good of life ingredient in her pregnancy and established a relationship with the fetus that is marked by respect for its life. She shows by her care and nurture of the fetus in pregnancy that she regards this developing form of human life as if it were already a person, and she does all she can to assure its well-being. In the moral relation between pregnant woman and fetus, the fetus receives from the woman a promise that it will be brought to term, and that promise is evidence that a moral relation between mother and fetus has been established. The woman is free of any pressing moral conflict leading her to determine that her pregnancy is unwanted. In such an instance of pregnancy—which is, one hopes, the rule and not the exception—such a woman would honor this moral relation, this covenant of promise, with the fetus such that she would most likely grieve at the loss of the fetus in a spontaneous abortion or miscarriage. Taking seriously the duties of tending to this moral relation, such a woman would seek to protect that fetus by attending to its nutritional needs and all other aspects of her prenatal condition, so as to enhance the possibility that the fetus will not only grow and develop, but flourish.[7]

By focusing on the moral institution of promise-keeping, the fetus' status as a developing biological form of human life becomes secondary as a moral issue to the moral relation into which the pregnant woman voluntarily enters to honor her promise to the fetus. She makes that promise in full partnership with the fetus, expecting nothing in return, knowing that the fetus is immature, not yet an actual person or able to act as if it possessed the many (neocortical-related) properties we ascribe to persons (i.e, self-consciousness, language capabilities, relationality, a sense of time, curiosity, etc.). The promise to bring to term confers upon the fetus the moral status of person, however, for at the point when the mother makes this promise with her relational partner (the fetus), she acts toward it as if it were a person, and the moral community supports her in that conferral of moral status.

Just abortion includes as a necessary criterion that *an abortion cannot be justifiably performed after a pregnant woman has made a promise to the fetus, explicitly or implicitly, to bring it to term.* The question is naturally asked, When does a pregnant woman actually make that promise? And that question leads to another: At what point in pregnancy can it be assumed that a prospective mother has made an implicit promise to the fetus, so that the fetus' life ought to be protected even if the pregnant woman should decide that she would prefer to abort it?

There is no hard and fast answer to the first question, simply because a woman may enter into moral relation with her fetus at different moments in her pregnancy, and those different moments will correspond to different stages of fetal development. When she would make such a promise would depend, as an empirical matter, on such variables as how soon after conception a woman knows she is pregnant—it could be a day, or a week, or a month, or even later. (Medical ethicists cite a well-known case of an obese pregnant woman who went into labor having never realized that she was pregnant.) But the promise a mother makes to her fetus to bring it to term can occur as early as that first moment when a woman knows she is pregnant—and for many women this is the case. Pregnancy is a good of life in which many women and couples seek to participate. Those couples who have experienced fertility problems and who find themselves suddenly and joyously pregnant would be ideal candidates for this revised version of person-from-conception thinking. That is, the promise to bring to term is made as soon as one knows one is pregnant.

But what is the relevance of the promise-keeping criterion to unwanted pregnancy, and when does the idea of an implicit promise come into play in an unwanted pregnancy?

If a pregnancy is unwanted, a woman withholds entering into a moral relation with the fetus and does not promise to bring it to term. If the other conditions of just abortion are satisfied, the refusal to extend the promise to bring to term would make the abortion option a morally permissible option. But one cannot indefinitely suspend judgment on the question of whether the pregnancy is wanted or not. The biological fact that a fetus is growing and developing becomes relevant to a moral determination in the following sense. If a mother allows the fetus to grow and develop for a period of time, she is moving toward making an implicit promise to bring the fetus to term. The issue then is at what point in fetal development does the broader moral community have an interest in seeing to it that the implicit promise a mother makes to the fetus is respected and enforced.

The U.S. Supreme Court in *Roe v. Wade* established this cut-off point at twelve weeks, the end of the first trimester. During this time, abortions on demand were allowed. As a mother moved into the second trimester, restrictions on abortion and medical involvement in making the decision for abortion were deemed essential for protecting a legitimate state interest in the fetus' life. The trimester scheme was based on various considerations, including medical safety, but the question of the cut-off point beyond which abortions ought to be restricted was not settled by this scheme. Critics of *Roe* often cite the fact that second-trimester abortions are not hard to come by; and the increased incidence of medical complications in second-trimester abortions is upheld as a reason for restriction when one reads the following statement from *A Clinical Manual of Gynecology*: "Because of the many problems associated with second-trimester termination of pregnancy, including medicolegal and psychosocial as well as purely medical, *such procedures are best done in facilities where they are performed routinely*. In such a setting an experienced staff will avoid many of the errors experienced by a staff exposed to these procedures on an intermittent basis."[8]

The idea that second-trimester abortions are routine in some facilities counts against the idea that medical reasons, including that of the mother's safety, would suffice to restrict abortions to the first trimester, when safer methods of abortion can be used with less risk to the patient.[9] But even pointing out that second-trimester abortions are in some facilities routine and hence not more dangerous to the mother than continued pregnancy (see criterion 4 in chapter 4) begs the moral question. For the moral question is not simply about medical procedures—although medical safety is a factor, as we note in criterion 4—but about the pregnant woman's relation to the fetus. Is there a point in pregnancy when one can reasonably assume that the pregnant woman has made a promise to bring the fetus to term and beyond which aborting the fetus is morally impermissible?

As a moral rather than a biological matter, if a pregnancy has gone twenty weeks one can say that an implicit promise to bring the fetus to term has been made, and that aborting it beyond that point, unless the woman's life is in danger, is not morally appropriate.

I choose the twenty-week period as a cut off because at that point a case could be made, as Peter Wenz has made it,[10] that the fetus, although still immature, has developed such that it is closer to resembling a newborn than it is to resembling a conceptus or even a young fetus. Keep in mind that as a practical matter, newborns are admitted into the moral community without controversy, so that if a fetus is so developed that it is more like a newborn than not, that fact of resemblance could be considered morally relevant.

The prospect of aborting seven-month-old fetuses on demand is shocking and morally repugnant; and that repugnance is generated from a recognition that so many things have occurred in fetal development by seven months that the fetus is no longer akin to the original zygote but more akin to a newborn. All things being equal, a seven-month fetus should be admitted into the moral community and afforded protection by that community without undue controversy.[11] At twenty weeks a fetus has in place a neocortex and its lungs are developing; 10 percent of premature babies at twenty weeks can be expected to survive premature birth. Fetal development has advanced sufficiently at twenty weeks to allow us to say reasonably that the fetus is no longer young and possessed of a vague sense of potentiality for being a person—the kind of potentiality that one could ascribe to every fertilized egg, even those eggs that wind up sloughing off the uterine wall without a woman ever realizing she carried, however briefly, a fertilized ovum. [12] At twenty weeks, however, the sense of potentiality is immediate—the physical structures that will support and sustain life and make possible full human life and personhood are already in place, especially the neocortex, even though neuronal circuitry in the upper layers of the cerebral cortex thought to be necessary for higher mental functions are not present and operational. [13] The conclusion one could draw, then, is that because of the resemblance to acknowledged members of the moral community (i.e., newborns), the fetus at twenty weeks ought to be extended the same protections we extend to those newborns.

Beyond this, we need to consider an even more relevant fact. By twenty weeks into a pregnancy, a woman has had sufficient, even ample, time to determine whether she will promise the fetus that she will bring it to term. The pregnancy, if normal, is at midpoint, and beyond this, the fetus is only more possessed of those properties that obtain with respect to newborns, including an increased likelihood of survivability.

The twenty-week cut-off period is an extreme limit, and clearly any justified abortion ought to be performed earlier rather than later. But by putting forth a twenty-week cut-off period, I mean to say that if a decision for abortion has not been reached by this time and an abortion actually performed, then the moral community has an obligation to infer from the pregnant woman's behavior that she has made a tacit promise to bring the fetus to term; and the moral community thus can claim a right to enforce that promise even if the pregnant woman should change her mind. She has made an implicit promise to the fetus to bring it to term, and ordinarily she ought to honor that promise. A just abortion cannot normally be performed beyond this twenty-week period, not only because the fetus has now come to resemble a recognized member of the moral community (newborn) or because the medical complications of abortion have increased and may make continued pregnancy safer than abortion. An abortion ought not to be performed beyond this point on the moral grounds that the fetus can now be assumed to be protected by an implicit promise that the mother has made to bring it to term.

Were a woman to elect to abort her seven-month-old fetus, would that constitute murder? Again, the situation must be taken into account, for it is possible that a complication of some kind has arisen that might render abortion a morally justified option. For example, the mother's life could be endangered by proceeding with the pregnancy, or a handicap might be detected that is so grave that abortion might be deemed in the fetus' best interest (e.g., anencephaly). But lacking any such extenuating circumstances, just abortion would generally oppose such late-term abortions, evaluating an abortion at that point in pregnancy as morally impermissible.

That moral evaluation, however, does not justify evaluating even a late-term abortion as murder. Murder identifies a killing of human persons that cannot be justified—use of the term murder is absolutist in its moral (as opposed to legal) evaluation. A seven-month-old fetus, even though its life is protected as if it were a person, cannot be said actually to be a person. It may resemble a newborn, but the fact of its resemblance to a newborn is also a way of pointing out that it is not yet a newborn and not the newborn's moral equivalent in the eyes of the moral community. There are ambiguities that surround even a late-term abortion. Those ambiguities, which reflect metaphysical issues about the meaning and moment of personhood and an ontology of selfhood, are such that one is not entitled to make the kind of morally absolutist claim that is involved anytime murder is used to describe the moral meaning of a killing. The unborn fetus is not a person by virtue of possessing realized intrinsic attributes or characteristics, but it receives protection as if it were a person from a moral community that wishes to care for and protect it. It resembles a newborn, but it is not a newborn. The killing violates the implicit promise the pregnant woman makes to bring the fetus to term—and such an abortion ought not to be performed, morally speaking.

By continuing to hold up ambiguities involved in the ontology of person, I am not saying that aborting a seven-month-old fetus is therefore permissible and non-controversial. The point is that such an abortion can be said with some assurance to be wrong and impermissible, even despicable, morally speaking. But it would be wrong for reasons that take into account the moral relation of the mother (and the moral community) to the unborn fetus—and not for reasons that are morally absolutist and unconditional, which is what murder implies.[14]

This sixth and last criterion of just abortion holds that abortion is eligible for moral justification if the abortion is performed *prior to the promise* a pregnant woman makes to her fetus to bring it to term. This shifts the moral meaning of abortion away from developmental characteristics of the fetus and from the need to impute moral meaning to particular points of fetal development. Rather, moral meaning is shifted to the moral relation of a pregnant woman (and the moral community) to a fetus. Abortions that are performed after a reasonable time has passed in the pregnancy are unjustified because that time during which the fetus grows and develops is the basis for inferring that the pregnant woman is making an implicit promise to the fetus to bring it to term, to extend to it a promise of life and membership in the moral community. Under just abortion theory, abortions ought not to be performed after that reasonable time, but always earlier in the pregnancy, as soon as one is reasonably sure that the pregnancy is not wanted and the other conditions for just abortion are satisfied. Women who may consider abortion ought not to postpone their decision unduly, for doing so increases the prospect that the promise to bring to term can be reasonably and even fairly inferred by all the behaviors that would seem to express tacit consent to such a promise.

# Conclusion

## JUST ABORTION: A SUMMARY OF THE ARGUMENT

Just abortion, as I have argued for it in these pages, accepts, affirms, and endorses a moral presumption against abortion. It also accepts that ours is an imperfect and complex world, where moral problems arise in the experience of peoples' lives. Just abortion acknowledges that in this imperfect world, for various reasons, not all pregnancies are greeted with enthusiasm and joy. In those situations where a pregnancy is determined to be un-wanted or undesired, abortion presents a possible option for re-sponding to the unwanted pregnancy; but the abortion option, according to just abortion theory, always presents a moral prob-lem. It does so because one faces the prospect of killing a devel-oping form of human life when the good of life ingredient in pregnancy is protected by a strong and abiding moral presump-tion against abortion. The moral presumption against abortion so values the good of life ingredient in pregnancy that it pre-sumes that pregnancies will go to term, that they will not be terminated, and that the good of life will be honored—unless good and sufficient reasons can be offered in particular situations to justify lifting that presumption. My purpose has been to ar-ticulate that moral presumption and then set out conditions that would, if satisfied, allow us reasonably to render a judgment that a particular abortion could be morally justified. By implication, those prospective abortions that do not satisfy these conditions would not be morally permissible.

Just abortion holds to the moderate view that some abortions are permissible and others not. Because ours is an imperfect world and moral absolutism distorts the ambiguities and uncertainties that surround the abortion issue, just abortion rejects absolutist solutions that fail to confront abortion as if it were a moral problem. Just abortion provides a structural guide for thinking though particular instances where abortion might be considered. It imposes moral restraints through conditions that seek to preserve the moral presumption against abortion. Yet it also opens the possibility that in those circumstances where the good of life ingredient in pregnancy is placed in conflict with other goods such that the pregnancy is evaluated as unwanted, certain specific conditions would allow one reasonably and justifiably to lift the moral presumption against abortion. Those six necessary and sufficient conditions are summarized as follows:

1. A just abortion must be based upon a determination that the pregnancy is not wanted, and the determination must be made by competent authority.
2. A just cause for seeking the abortion must be established. Determining just cause must take into account not only individual behaviors giving rise to an unwanted pregnancy, but also issues of social complicity and corporate responsibility. Just cause must attend to the complex of causal issues, both individual and corporate, that affects the situation of women who find themselves having to consider abortion when, all things being equal, they would if possible, as responsible and rational agents, act to prevent pregnancy when pregnancy is not desired.
3. For an abortion to be just, it must be considered a last resort to the condition of unwanted pregnancy. This criterion insists that the moral problems associated with the option of bringing an unwanted fetus to term and giving the newborn up for adoption be confronted and not dismissed as obviously non-problematic morally.
4. The abortion cannot pose a greater medical risk to the pregnant woman than continued pregnancy. This criterion must be considered in conjunction with condition 6, for the longer a pregnancy continues, the less certain medical success becomes. The pregnant woman's body undergoes con-

tinual change, and the methods for abortion become more difficult and even risky from a medical point of view. While diagnosis and prognosis for medical success must be dealt with on an individual basis, this condition of just abortion requires that if it is determined that a woman faces more medical risk by having an abortion than by continuing a pregnancy, then concern for the well-being of the pregnant woman ought to dictate that the abortion not proceed.

5. A just abortion will not summarily sacrifice those values that the unwanted pregnancy has placed in conflict with the good of life. While abortion involves a killing, and the killing of a fetus is never a good to be sought in itself, the killing can be justified if the values being preserved and protected at the expense of the loss of that fetal life out-weigh in particular circumstances the value of preserving that life. Societal concerns once again become relevant because just abortion requires that even if in a particular circumstance the moral presumption against abortion is lifted, the lifting of it must not in itself lead to a more general subversion of the value of life for the individual or for the society in which the abortion is performed.

6. Rather than dealing with the intrinsic properties of per-sonhood that some argue attach at certain points in bio-logical development and which thus provide protection to the fetus, just abortion makes a moral claim that abortions can only be performed prior to the promise a pregnant woman makes to bring the fetus to life. A cut-off point is set at around twenty weeks, and ordinarily abortions would not be justifiable beyond that time. Although physiological development and biological evolution are relevant to lo-cating a point beyond which abortions ought not be per-formed, the focus of this last criterion is not biological but moral. This criterion seeks to establish a moral basis for determining when in a pregnancy an abortion is eligible for moral justification and when it is not.

These criteria stand as moral barriers to abortion and function to preserve the moral presumption against abortion. If satisfied, however, they provide rational and morally justifiable reasons for lifting the moral presumption against abortion.

## OTHER ISSUES: SOCIAL POLICY, CAPITAL PUNISHMENT, RELIGION

Three other issues relevant to the theory of just abortion must be addressed, however briefly. The first pertains to social policy and the implication of just abortion for political decision-making. The second issue is that of capital punishment, for I must explain why the theory of just abortion does not lead to the conclusion that capital punishment can also be a form of just(ified) killing. And the last issue pertains to the question of religion and faith and how just abortion, as a moral theory that does not draw explicitly on Scripture or religious tradition—at least as I have presented it—is relevant and expressive of a faith perspective.

### JUST ABORTION AND SOCIAL POLICY

If some abortions are morally permissible and others are not, then social policy must be directed toward creating a political, legal, social, and medical environment that allows those abortions deemed to be morally permissible to proceed. Social policy aimed at prohibiting abortion on the assumption that all abortions are morally impermissible must be opposed as absolutist, as repressive in subjugating women's humanity to fetal humanity, and, as with all absolutist perspectives, as ultimately contradictory.[1]

Just abortion therefore endorses, and assumes, a pro-choice social policy. I understand pro-choice to be the moderate social policy option most consistent with the just abortion claim that some—perhaps many—abortions are morally justifiable. Making room in the social and political environment so that women seeking abortions can receive them raises another issue, however. Then the question arises about restricting abortions not only morally but legally, in terms of social policy. Can abortions be restricted under just abortion theory?

The answer is yes. The abortion option in just abortion theory is not to be thought of as an absolute, unrestricted right. Unrestricted abortion flies in the face of just abortion theory, the purpose of which is to articulate conditions that would allow one morally to justify an exception to a generally recognized moral presumption against abortion. That presumption holds in place a restrictive abortion position, namely, that only those abortions that can be morally justified ought to be performed and only up to a certain point in gestation (around twenty weeks at the outside). Just abortion, which always demands justification for any particular abortion, is a theory of restriction, although unlike a legal decision like *Roe v. Wade*, it is a theory of moral restriction rather than legal restriction.

Restricting abortions through social policy decisions, however, is clearly in line with a moderate approach. *Roe v. Wade* restricted abortions, allowing unrestricted abortion only during the first trimester of pregnancy. Societies as moral communities have an interest in protecting and promoting the good of life, and the morally moderate position advanced by just abortion theory acknowledges that interest and seeks to guide moral decision-making in relation to it. However, restrictions, rather than serving the absolutist goal of prohibition, which is unjust, ought to be devised to serve the goal of rendering every abortion a just abortion. Just abortion affirms that women who have employed just abortion thinking, and who have established good and sound moral reasons for lifting the moral presumption against abortion, ought to be free in their particular societies to receive a medically safe abortion, although generally not beyond twenty weeks into pregnancy. Any other restrictions should be accepted only if they help individual women and couples—and even society itself—confront the moral problem of abortion and resolve that problem in given contexts in such a way that the mother's well-being is protected and advanced, and a responsible, just decision is made with respect to terminating a developing form of human life.

Endorsing a pro-choice social policy assumes that the moral requirements that would allow an abortion to proceed have been satisfied; that moral obstructions have been removed; and that moral objections have been met with arguments more compelling than the objection itself. This response to moral issues clears the way so that those persons who are considering the abortion option in actual situations of unwanted pregnancy can then decide whether to proceed with the medical procedure involved in abortion. In that just abortion theory establishes a moral framework for testing the justifiability of a prospective abortion, it establishes a means whereby persons can determine which abortions are morally justifiable and which are not. Because this theory avoids absolutism and does not prejudge any particular situation in the light of a value absolute, just abortion advances a morally moderate approach to the abortion question.

Once the moral permissibility of abortion has been established by means of just abortion theory, social policy must lend support to the moral evaluation by seeing to it that the medical procedure itself is not hampered or impeded. No unnecessary risks to the health and safety of the pregnant woman should be permitted. As a social policy matter, this is what endorsing a pro-choice position means. It means that if at least some abortions are morally permissible, then society must make it possible for individuals to exercise their abortion option safely and without undue medical or psychological burdens.

This social policy implication of just abortion theory will of course be distressing to pro-life supporters who want to see abortion prohibited. But prohibiting abortions at the level of social policy would reflect an absolutist perspective that equates abortion with murder. We lack a societal consensus about that particular evaluation of the moral meaning of abortion, and I see no prospect of ever achieving such a consensus. There will always be in a society that values life a reluctance to assign to a developing embryo or fetus the same moral status as a pregnant woman, so that in a life-and-death conflict one would have no moral basis for determining which life is of greater value. To equate abortion with murder would require such an evaluation, and reasonable people, whether mothers, prospective mothers, or just people willing to employ the Golden Rule, would be reluctant to equate fetal humanity with that of a mother, whose status in the moral community is not—and ought not to be—in question.

Not only does a societal consensus about the moral meaning of abortion not exist, and never will, such a consensus *ought not to exist*. It would express a society's collective determination that moral certainty can be, and actually has been, achieved on this issue. That conclusion would be purchased at a terrible price. Claiming moral certainty and prohibiting abortions on the basis of that claim would require a society at large to dispense with evaluations of abortion that present value conflicts and moral complexities. It would require the elimination of interpretive problems and uncertainties, which could lead to deceptively simple and misleading moral evaluations. That result would offend against the good of practical reasonableness that persons committed to the values of intellectual honesty and respect for truth-telling would, as members of the moral community, want to observe. Interpreting abortion as if it were not fraught with moral complexity would so distort the issue that the description itself would become a legitimate target for serious moral inquiry and evaluation.

Given the fracture that abortion has created in contemporary American society, one can imagine consensus on the moral meaning of abortion being achieved only by coercion and deception, and being sustained only by individual and corporate acts of self-deception. Such means do not promote visions of the good but wound the good and attack the foundations of the moral life. The attempt to sustain an absolutist moral position through immoral means leads to the terrible ethical contradiction of doing evil so that good might result. Not only would moral philosophies of various kinds oppose such a view, since such a contradiction offends against the good of practical reasonableness, but it is worth pointing out that Christianity, which—in a purely descriptive sense—allows for a diversity of opinion on the abortion issue, has long opposed this contradiction in its moral tradition, even holding it up for scorn and ridicule in the New Testament (Rom. 3:8).[2]

To summarize: A just abortion theory will assume a social policy position that refuses to prohibit abortions because at least some abortions will be morally justifiable. This position should not be perceived as endorsing the view that abortion is a positive good we ought to promote. Neither does it allow us to justify any or all abortions on moral grounds. It simply creates the necessary room in society so that abortion can be confronted as a moral problem, with society refusing on the one hand to play the role of moral absolutist while accepting on the other the practical and morally defensible position that some abortions are morally permissible and others are not.

## JUST ABORTION AND CAPITAL PUNISHMENT

Because I uphold a moral presumption for protecting the good of life but offer, in the name of non-absolutism, exceptions to that presumption, a necessary implication seems to follow on the issue of capital punishment. That implication would be this: that the kind of argument I have presented actually endorses capital punishment because it could be said that executing a person for taking another's life satisfies the moral community's sense of justice without subscribing to a morally absolutist position on the question of life. If the state observes a moral presumption against the taking of life and accepts an obligation to respect and promote life, the case could be made that that moral presumption can be justly overturned in certain specific and highly restricted situations. Certain crimes could be determined to be exceptions to the moral presumption that the state ought to defend and protect life and not kill persons who commit crimes. Murder would be such an exception to that moral presumption, and executing murderers would be a justified, non-absolutist exception to the presumption against the state participating in the willful killing of its citizens.

I have written on the capital punishment issue elsewhere[3] and have provided both religious and moral reasons why capital punishment ought to be opposed. Undoubtedly some persons oppose capital punishment because they are absolutists with regard to the question of the value of life, and they oppose capital punishment for much the same reason they oppose abortion—that it is always morally wrong to deprive human beings of the good of life.

Just abortion, as a non-absolutist approach to moral analysis and evaluation, does raise the capital punishment question in a new way, since it could be argued that having eschewed moral absolutism, capital punishment simply expresses an exception to a prevailing moral presumption that persons ought not to be killed. Just abortion could, one might argue, translate into a theory of just execution, where, in certain circumscribed situations, certain persons—murderers, say—can be justifiably killed; that is, the moral presumption against the state killing its citizens can be justifiably lifted in this specific situation.

Although this kind of argument would allow one to say that just execution is a proposal for a non-absolutist perspective, I construe the moral absolutism issue differently with regard to capital punishment. Just abortion does not translate into just execution because the absolute in question is not that directed toward the protection of the good of life, but the absolute power of the state to determine guilt or innocence with such certainty, and from a position of such absolute moral authority and non-complicity in criminal behavior, that it could impose an absolute and irrevocable punishment that would deprive persons of a basic and fundamental good of life.

In order for the state to proceed with an execution, it must assume the power to ascertain the moral meaning of the person's crime (which the state-as-terrorist does not always confine to murder, but sometimes extends to include simple opposition to the absolute authority of the state: witness capital punishment in Iran, China, South Africa). It establishes that moral meaning with moral certainty, then dispenses justice on the basis of absolute epistemological certainty. That certainty is absolute because once the execution is performed, the loss of life is irrevocable and the person is deprived of any chance to appeal injustices that may have occurred in the system that delivered the justice. The state proceeds in an execution as if error could not—and actually did not—occur, and that is an arrogation of power if one believes that the state is capable of making errors, of delivering unjust sentences, even of punishing innocent persons. Imposing death on fully endowed members of the moral community, even those who have been convicted of the heinous crime of murder, negates any such sense of human fallibility.

Where capital punishment is a tool of the state, the state has assumed a moral position of absolute authority in the power to impose death and prevent redress of injustice—absolute moral authority because it assumes no injustice could be delivered by the state.

Opposing capital punishment, then, does not on this argument represent a non-absolutist defense of the good of life, but opposition to an assumption by the state of absolute moral authority. Just abortion allows for the possibility of lifting a moral presumption that protects and promotes the good of life. However, one cannot, in analogy to just abortion, also say that this is how to conceive of capital punishment. One would say, rather, that just abortion arises in the face of certain moral uncertainties and opposes a moral absolutism with respect to the good of life. An opponent of capital punishment need not hold any kind of absolutism with respect to the good of life, and can still face moral uncertainties with respect to punishment of a murderer. But a murderer's status as a member of the moral community is not in doubt—a human embryo's status is. A murderer is still a person, a member of the moral community, and only an absolute moral authority could willfully and justifiably kill such a person for something that person did. The issue is whether the state should be invested with that kind of moral authority, or whether the authority ought to be reserved for something, or someone, more capable of delivering epistemologically and evaluatively certain judgments about moral meaning. God, for instance, would be a traditional construct or repository for such an investiture of moral absoluteness. The question then is whether one wants the state to fill a role most appropriately played by God.

The point of comparison between just abortion and capital punishment is not that both constitute exceptions to a general moral presumption against killing, but how each responds to moral absolutism. Just abortion and opposition to capital punishment are generated from the same desire to oppose moral absolutism. Both positions resist, in the name of moral moderation, any claims to absolute moral certainty. Supporters of capital punishment assume a moral absolutist stance the same way moral absolutists on the abortion issue assume it.

It is sometimes argued that opponents of capital punishment who are also pro-choice on the abortion issue are inconsistent in that stance. This is not so inconsistent as it looks, for both positions stand against human pretensions to absolute certainty. The deeper and, I believe, unresolvable contradiction arises in the position of those who oppose all abortions and who then support the death penalty; and it is no mere coincidence that many pro-life absolutists also support, as absolutists, capital punishment. Such persons can only do that because they claim absolute certainty from an absolute moral authority: they know when and how a fetus is a person so that they can extend it absolute protection in pregnancy; and they claim to know absolutely that an individual convicted of a crime against the moral community is unworthy as a moral being of holding on to the basic good of life.[4]

Whatever the source of that certainty, and I would call it religious since there are no commonly accepted secular standards for making those epistemological determinations, it is the *absolutism*—and the human pretension to be able to act absolutely, infallibly, with complete moral certainty about moral meaning—that is of moral concern. Opposing capital punishment does not necessarily commit one to non-resistance or pacifism or otherwise rob one of possible justifications for taking human life in other kinds of circumstances and situations. What opposing capital punishment means, morally speaking, is that one is standing against a value absolutism that is destructive of the goods of life, including the good of practical reasonableness, which, when lost, places one in danger of becoming a fanatic. Moral absolutism, as I have stressed throughout these pages, is the enemy of practical reasonableness and must be avoided if the moral life is going to flourish in humane community.

In short, a theory of just execution cannot be developed on the just abortion model because any execution will have to assume a moral absolutism on the part of the executor (the state) that is unwarranted because of the epistemological and moral certainty that would have to be assumed before an execution could proceed. For all the ambiguity and uncertainty that surrounds the developing embryo or young fetus when considering abortion, we must affirm emphatically and categorically that no such ambiguity surrounds a convicted criminal, whose moral status in the community is never removed because of something he or she has done, however heinous.

Just abortion is an argument against moral absolutism. Opposition to capital punishment, rather than being a morally pure cause that seeks to uphold the value of the good of life without exception—this would constitute a clear contradiction with just abortion principles—is actually opposition to another kind of absolutism, namely, that assumed by the state as it seeks to arrogate to itself the absolute moral authority it requires to condemn persons to death and then proceed with killing them. Arguing that just abortion provides an argument to justify capital punishment, then, fails. Opposing capital punishment, rather than expressing a value absolutism with respect to the good of life, is set in opposition to value absolutism. Opposing capital punishment is consistent with just abortion in that both approaches oppose moral absolutism and the epistemological and moral certainty that such absolutism naturally assumes and logically entails.

## RELIGION AND FAITH

The reader who has been seeking in these pages a theological perspective on the abortion issue is no doubt disappointed that my discussion has been confined to ethics, with religion only tangentially discussed. That, of course, was intentional. Because my major concern was to address the moral issue at stake in abortion, and to reiterate the respects in which abortion is a moral problem, I undertook the book as a work in moral philosophy rather than constructive theology.

Religion-based disagreements about abortion will always be with us. In a free society, a broader, non-sectarian basis for moral community must be recognized. The foundations of value for that community, and for a moral discourse available for all to use, even if a particular religious view prohibits some from doing so, are both necessary and vital to maintaining and promoting a community that is, in the end, a moral community based on shared concerns, interests, and values. One more theological discussion of abortion, as much as it might serve to articulate particular theological perspectives, would not address this larger moral community. Neither would such a discussion remind it that in the face of differing theological or religious perspectives on abortion, the moral community, if it seeks bonds of unity in broader value concerns based on secular modes of analysis and justification, must not endorse one particular theological view over against another. It must not do so if the moral community itself is concerned to protect divergent and conflicting religious and theological viewpoints.

I have sought, then, to address the broader moral community with a moral argument rather than a religious argument. What is needed on so divisive an issue as abortion is not one more view that could be dismissed as sectarian or tribalistic or, to use the word I have used here, absolutist. Rather, what is needed is respectful public conversation grounded in a common moral discourse.

It is imperative that we not ignore the profound role that religious thought plays in the abortion issue. While no one would deny that religious perspectives on the abortion issue are widely divergent, the religious dimension of the issue reaches into the very heart of the moral problematic. Recognizing this is important for how we proceed with our public, legal, and constitutional debate over abortion. I support the argument that in the absence of any kind of secular standard that convincingly determines fetal humanity such that the fetus can be admitted non-controversially into the moral community, at least until that point in development (around twenty weeks) at which it comes to resemble an accepted member of the moral community (a newborn), whatever perspective one holds on the moral status of the conceptus, zygote, embryo, or young fetus has the character of a religiously determined evaluation. This was a point explicitly made by Supreme Court justice John Paul Stevens in his *Webster v. Reproductive Health Services* decision dissent. There he wrote that "unless the religious view that a fetus is a 'person' is adopted . . . there is a fundamental and well-recognized difference between a fetus and a human being." The Missouri statute in *Webster* was based on state legislature findings that "the life of each human being begins at conception" and that "unborn children have protectable interests in life, health and well-being" (quoted in Stevens). This led Stevens to comment:

> If the views of St. Thomas [Aquinas] were held as widely today as they were in the Middle Ages, and if a state legislature were to enact a statute prefaced with a "finding" that female life begins 80 days after conception and male life begins 40 days after conception [which was St. Thomas' view], I have no doubt that this Court would promptly conclude that such an endorsement of a particular religious tenet is violative of the Establishment Clause.
>
> In my opinion the difference between that hypothetical statute and Missouri's preamble reflects nothing more than a difference in theological doctrine.[5]

As Peter Wenz has commented on this passage: "Stevens' cogent objection to the statute rests on his claim that, unlike other laws that coincide with religious views, Missouri's preamble has *no secular justification*."[6] It is not unusual for religious and secular views to coincide, for both secular and religious goals are served when persons observe religious laws that prohibit theft and murder, for instance, or that promote helping the poor. But in his evaluation of the question of abortion and fetal humanity Stevens points out that there is no secular justification for a finding that personhood begins at conception—even if certain people for various reasons (i.e., religious reasons) believe that to be the case.

In the absence of a secular justification for determination, perhaps scientifically or in some other way that achieves broad societal consensus, a belief that personhood should be ascribed at conception constitutes a religious belief—that is, it is a belief that can be held but cannot be justified by secular modes of justification. In that case, arguing about fetal humanity is somewhat akin to arguing about the difference between infant baptism and baptism by consent (or believer's baptism), with Baptists, Mennonites, and Disciples of Christ representing a pro-choice position and supporters of infant baptism (Roman

Catholics, Lutherans, and other Protestants) for doctrinal and dogmatic reasons not respecting choice as crucial for the delivery of the sacrament. Any kind of comparison here goes to the moral issue of what a society committed to free religious expression *ought* to allow and endorse. And just as society ought not to impose or establish a religious view on the religious question of baptism, for which no secular justification exists, neither should it impose, as a legal dictum or constitutional axiom, a view with respect to religious beliefs about fetal humanity that cannot be justified according to secular standards.

If the question of fetal humanity is a religious question—at least until that point in fetal development is reached at which the fetus is widely accepted as belonging to the moral community, then it is inappropriate for the government to impose on me a religious belief I do not share.[7] If the question of fetal humanity before twenty weeks is a religious question, the religious beliefs ought to be respected in their plurality and not determined by governmental authority pronouncing on the society at large a belief about fetal humanity that is for all intents and purposes, a religious belief. I agree with those who argue that *Roe v. Wade* was inadequately constructed as a legal argument. Accepting that stronger, more explicit arguments ought to prevail over weaker, implicit arguments, justifying abortion rights on First Amendment religious freedom grounds—particularly with the prohibition that government shall make no law establishing religion—seems to me the explicit and stronger argument to make, and a fundamental right to privacy an implicit, hence a weaker, constitutional argument.[8]

The role that religion plays in abortion is, therefore, a vital one, and recognizing that in a free society citizens are guaranteed constitutional protection from governmental attempts to establish religious beliefs is crucial to the operation of the U.S. Constitution and the functioning of a pluralistic and free society. Given the differing positions religious people can have on the question of fetal humanity, the government's role is to so protect religious freedom that no one view ever becomes established as an official view. The government, therefore, must not only protect persons who hold the position my denomination, the

United Church of Christ, has pronounced in its General Synod, but, as a matter of constitutional protection, it must protect the civil rights of those members of the denomination who disagree with it (such as the Biblical Witness Fellowship). The Constitution must make room for Roman Catholics who follow the papal directives of "Humanae Vitae" and also for pro-choice Catholics; it must protect the views of Jews, Moslems, and Zen Buddhists on fetal humanity; and it must protect the right of citizens to hold religious beliefs that are even more conservative than those of the Roman Catholic church—for instance, those who subscribe to the Shinto belief that an aborted fetus will return to place a curse on its mother.

It is important to keep in mind how beliefs about so critical an issue as fetal humanity are necessarily bound by beliefs that cannot be justified by secular means, and that as religious beliefs, their protection by the Constitution is vital.

Another connection between abortion and religion is explicitly theological, and, again, the reader of these pages has not been invited into theological discussion. Let me reiterate that I sought to address abortion as a moral problem. I did so because those whose moral views on abortion are grounded in religious beliefs must still present their views in a pluralistic context where those beliefs are not shared. In the absence of such a culture-wide sharing of beliefs, how does one construct moral meaning on the abortion issue such that one crosses the beliefs put forth from particular religious communities? In arguing for a just abortion theory in a secular mode, I sought to evade an explicitly religious clash of absolutes to highlight the foundation for a moderated mode of analysis and argumentation. My hope was that this kind of approach might lead those of us who are theologians and religious thinkers to reconsider how our views of personhood, grounded as they are in religious belief and theological conceptions of the human, have contributed to a distressing societal problem, namely, the fact that many today are unable to address abortion as if it were truly a moral problem. In our current cultural context the premise of this study—namely, that abortion *is* a moral problem—has to be argued for and not assumed; and I continue to hold that because of religious views, many who confront the abortion issue do not see it as a moral problem, but as an issue about which the moral meaning is clear. I deny that such clarity exists, or that it ought to exist.

By avoiding explicit theological discussion, I am not disclaiming religious or theological interest. I would even offer that this work has arisen from theological reflection. The reader familiar with religious ethics in the Western traditions will undoubtedly recognize the influence of that tradition on many facets of the just abortion argument. The religious or theological background for the philosophical perspectives offered here could be filled in without difficulty. Let me share briefly how that could be done.

For instance, the discussion about the goods of life could be attached to a theology of creation, where the goodness recognized in the various goods of life, including life itself, has been determined, in the first instance, by God's own act of divine valuation and interpretation. Whereas the goods of life are recognizable as good to reason, one could posit through a faith perspective that the reason they are good is because God, who is good, made them, necessarily made them good, and then recognized them as good. Reason, which is the image of God within us, cannot, except by perverseness, do differently. Valuation of the goods of life as good, therefore, is grounded in God's own valuation and in the acts of valuation we are able to perform as beings who bear God's image (reason). The goods of life, then, can be grounded in a theology of creation.

Another issue critical to this discussion is moral presumptions. Moral presumptions could likewise be considered grounded in a model of analysis and interpretation of moral issues found throughout sacred Scripture. Consider the moral presumption against killing. In the Old Testament, one could consider instances where God prohibits killing—in the sacrifice of Isaac (Gen. 22), for example, or in the giving of the fifth of the Ten Commandments (Exod. 20); or in the prohibition against taking the life of Cain after he murdered his brother (Gen. 4). The moral presumption against human beings killing other human beings is strong and clear.

Strong and clear as that moral presumption is, it is, as the Scriptures themselves reveal, only a presumption and not an absolute prohibition. For one must then consider incidents where this moral presumption is actually lifted, and sometimes for reasons that seem obscure morally or at least not necessarily morally compelling, even if religiously so. If Yahweh is the absolute moral evaluator or arbiter of moral meaning, one could simply say that when the absolute evaluator of moral meaning lifts the moral presumption against killing, that is all the justification required. At this point one is not subjecting God to a higher moral standard than God, but avowing God as the absolute moral standard and operating out of a divine command theory of ethics.

The Scriptures reveal that the presumption against killing human life is not an absolute prohibition but is lifted many times, even by Yahweh acting either directly or through intermediaries. We see the lifting of the moral presumption against taking human life in the stories of the Passover (Exod. 11–12); the flight from Egypt (Exod. 14); the rebellion of Korah (Num. 16); the punishment of golden calf worshipers (Exod. 31–32); the holy wars against the Amalekites (Gen. 14); and legal prescriptions requiring death as punishment (i.e., whoever strikes his mother or father), and so on.[9]

Moral presumptions as articulations of a moral non-absolutism are also apparent in the New Testament. In the New Testament Jesus acknowledges the force of legal teaching, although he also seeks to offer exceptions to legal proscriptions and prohibitions. One can look to Jesus as teaching fellow Jews to consider overruling the normative force of traditional teaching for reasons aimed at promoting the goods of life, with the result that he refuses to acknowledge various teachings of the tradition as absolute, even though they were interpreted as expressions of divine will. Thus does Jesus sanction pulling an animal in distress from a ditch on the Sabbath (Luke 14:5), lifting the traditional commandment to keep the Sabbath. Jesus does not abrogate the teaching or the commandment, but de-absolutizes it for human good, remarking at one point that the Sabbath was made for human beings and not human beings for the Sabbath (Mark 2.27). Whatever else it might be, this is a modeling of moral non-absolutism, even if one could argue, successfully I think, that it is a theological absolutism with respect to God's love—which, curiously, never expresses its absolute value as an absolute moral stricture or exceptionless prohibition.

The non-absolutism of the faith perspective shows itself to be applicable to the particular just abortion criteria—for example, the importance of the recognition in criterion 6 that human life develops and grows, and that moral meaning may evolve as a fetus grows and its moral status changes as it develops to the point where it more closely resembles a newborn than a fertilized egg. This idea that the fetus does not possess a static moral meaning from the moment of conception, but acquires moral meaning as it grows and develops and is accepted into moral relationship with the pregnant woman, springs from a vision of God's evolutionary creation. In the Genesis creation story, the human being is the final creature to emerge from God's creative act (Gen. 1:26)—this is itself an idea of evolutionary meaning. But there is an even more important notion of evolution in the Creation story, a notion relevant to moral development. It appears in the very simple portrayal of how the human being itself evolves toward moral understanding in the story of the Fall. The final part of the human being's evolution is the development of moral consciousness, and this appears shortly before expulsion from the Garden of Eden. A fetus before twenty weeks might be much like Adam in the garden: a being who is provided for, cared for, but who is also undeveloped morally and who experiences no shame or guilt in its paradise—this garden, this womb of God. But Adam grows and develops and comes to consciousness and even to moral understanding—and that precipitates the expulsion. The form of human life mythicized as Adam in the garden goes through growth and development from a point of unconscious innocence to a recognizable human being capable of guilt and desire, shame, remorse, and reformation. The idea that in pregnancy an immature form of human life grows and develops, and that this non-static picture of the human being as growing and developing has positive moral significance, resonates with modeling that occurs in the Scriptures.

In sum, then, for the person seeking theological explication of just abortion theory primarily through sacred Scripture, I would assert that scriptural warrants can be found for the values and perspectives advanced by the six criteria for just abortion.

Finally, the entire just abortion approach is itself modeled on a non-absolutist mode of moral analysis and presentation that has formal roots in St. Augustine and the development of the just war tradition. This is a tradition of non-absolutism that is the heritage of moral thought as it developed within, and was then transmitted through, the church.

I have not pursued this religious/theological tack since what most disturbs me about the abortion issue is not the theological absolutism that informs many moral positions but our failures in community to find common ground for moral discussion. On the broader constitutional religious issue, free societies dedicated to diverse and tolerant religious expression ought not to quash religious influence but make room for a plurality of religious views, refusing to let any one view prevail, especially on so complex and divisive an issue as fetal humanity. I am not so much concerned by the sociological fact that in a pluralistic society certain absolutist religious perspectives on the question of fetal humanity have been advanced and are seeking to influence social policy. What concerns me is the societal failure to identify the religious aspect of the abortion debate *as* religious. Were we to accomplish that reorientation, we could, as persons of goodwill, honor those diverse religious views in a moral community that is humane, respectful toward women, and critical of societal policies and priorities that fail to help people avoid unwanted pregnancies. Failure to address social and economic justice concerns—and particularly the problem of poverty—leads unfortunately to the perpetuation of those conditions and circumstances that prompt people to consider the abortion option, making abortion more, rather than less, likely an occurrence.

Most of all I am distressed that abortion is not addressed as if it were a true moral problem, for this indicates that on this issue we seem to have lost a common moral discourse. The abortion debate has revealed the extent to which we are losing a way to talk with one another about moral problems—on a common moral ground in a common language where people of goodwill can share common moral presumptions and agree to disagree about abortion. Differ as we might religiously, we all share certain values grounded in common goods of life. We are obligated to treat each other with respect, and we must find a way of conversing in a non-absolutist discourse that we all understand. We need to find a language that will acknowledge obligations to help the weak and helpless, that will guide moral decision-making, and that will resist the moral absolutism that, if unchecked, will suppress free inquiry, eliminate moral complexity, and quash theological dispute over moral problems that cannot be resolved except by fiat and arbitrariness. A free society, if it is to remain free, must accept this perhaps unwelcome but quite essential ambiguity concerning moral meaning.

# Notes

## INTRODUCTION

1. Jeffrey W. Ellis and Charles R. B. Beckman, A Clinical Manual of Gynecology (Norwalk, CT: Appleton-Century-Crofts, 1983), 256.
2. Ellis and Beckman, A Clinical Manual of Gynecology, 256.
3. I realize there are more than two major perspectives on the abortion issue, and that I run the risk of caricaturing, perhaps trivializing, the debate by pitting pro-choice against pro-life. A thorough treatment would have to account for the views of pro-life feminists, pro-choice Catholics, and certain persons who oppose abortion, even express sympathy with pro-life aims, yet who, for a variety of reasons—including for some the view that the greater good of basic societal functioning is at stake in the abortion debate—support a pro-choice social policy on the grounds that it is necessary for basic societal stability.
4. The talk referred to was published as "Abortion and the Conflict of Moral Presumptions," in Papers of the Craigville Theological Colloquy VI: Human Beginnings: Deciding about Life in the Presence of God (Craigville, MA: Craigville Conference Center, 1989): 20–23.
5. See my article "Applying 'Just War' Standards to the Gulf," Christian Science Monitor, Feb. 19, 1991, 19.
6. For background on just war theory see James F. Childress, "Just War Theories: The Bases, Interrelations, Priorities and Functions of Their Criteria," Theological Studies 39 (September 1978): 427–45; John P. Langan, "Elements of St. Augustine's Just War Theory," Journal of Religious Ethics 12, no. 1 (1984): 19–38; Paul Ramsey, The Just War: Force and Political Responsibility (New York: Charles Scribner's Sons, 1968); Thomas A. Shannon, ed., War or

*Peace? The Search for New Answers* (Maryknoll, NY: Orbis Press, 1982). Although I disagree strenuously with his policy applications, James Turner Johnson is one of the most knowledgeable scholars on just war theory. One should consult his *Just War Tradition and the Restraint of War: A Moral and Historical Inquiry* (Princeton: Princeton University Press, 1981) and *Can Modern War Be Just?* (New Haven: Yale University Press, 1984).

## CHAPTER 1. THE GOOD OF LIFE

1. The figures about the numbers of abortion in America are widely circulated; the world estimates were offered by Nancy Wallace of the Population Program of the Sierra Club and published by the Federal News Service, Thursday, July 9, 1992.
2. See Richard Selzer, *Mortal Lessons: Notes on the Art of Surgery* (New York: Simon and Schuster, 1974), 153–60.
3. By referring to moral communities, I do not mean that there are no value differences according to culture, nor even that a descriptive or sociological sense of moral relativism expresses a reality of human being and culture. But I do not accept moral relativism in the sense that there are no universal agreements, such as on the general value of life under discussion. What identifies a moral community—even a universal moral community prior to a specific moral community—is agreement on goods of life and the value of preserving and promoting those goods. Put another way, moral community is created by the bond of unity that is found in such basic affirmations as the value of life—that life is good and to be valued and promoted. Pro-life and pro-choice represent moral communities in conflict with each other. True though that may be, both moral communities affirm the basic good of the value of life and the fact that life is a good to be preserved and promoted. Moral communities divide into the pluralism of community over specific means of upholding and interpreting that good. One could say, then, that both pro-life and pro-choice are members of a general moral community that is bound together by an affirmation of the good of life, yet each has developed into a particular moral community because of differences regarding how that good is to be interpreted or set in relation to other goods with respect to the abortion issue.
4. For more on universal goods, see Germain Grisez and Russell Shaw, *Beyond the New Morality: The Responsibilities of Freedom*, 2d

ed. (Notre Dame: University of Notre Dame Press, 1974, 1980), 61–62. For another kind of perspective see Alan Gewirth, *Human Rights: Essays on Justification and Applications* (Chicago: University of Chicago Press, 1982): pp. 55–59. Gewirth identifies three kinds of goods necessary for human well-being: basic goods, which are the preconditions of action (life, physical integrity, mental equilibrium); nonsubtractive goods (being subjected to debilitating conditions in one's life, suffering broken promises, being lied to, cheated, or prevented from using one's resources to fulfill one's wants); and additive goods (those abilities and conditions that increase one's level of purpose-fulfillment, such as receiving an education, being free of discrimination, fear, and the like). Gewirth argues that humans have a right to these goods, and violation of the basic right to well-being constitutes a basic harm; while violations of nonsubtractive and additive rights constitute specific harms. The good of life, in Gewirth's terms, is a basic and universal right; and while I do not focus here on rights, a theory of rights, which is so much at play in the abortion essay, does appeal, in the first instance, to the very goods of life—the basic good of life itself—that are my focus.

5. This general framework of goods of life is from Grisez and Shaw, *Beyond the New Morality*, 61–62.

6. For a provocative essay on goodness and the human ability to recognize it, see Philip Hallie, "From Cruelty to Goodness," reprinted in Christina Hoff Sommers and Fred Sommers, eds., *Vice and Virtue in Everyday Life: Introductory Readings in Ethics*, 3d ed. (Fort Worth, TX: Harcourt Brace, 1993), 9–24. For more details, see Philip Hallie, *Lest Innocent Blood Be Shed: The Story of the Village of Le Chambon and How Goodness Happened There* (New York: Harper and Row, 1979).

7. This perspective on good as that which moves us is a familiar idea and has a long tradition in the west, from Socrates on. A most important contemporary defense of this view can be found in Charles Taylor, *Sources of the Self: The Making of the Modern Identity* (Cambridge: Harvard University Press, 1989).

8. Even self-consciousness can be lost, as in a coma. If irrecoverably lost, however, as in neocortical brain death, the value of biological functioning, which may not be itself impeded, is thrown into question. Decisions to terminate life support in brain-death cases are a manifestation not only of the preeminent value of life—for disconnection is not a trivial decision—but also an instance of how

the good of life is always a good in relation to other goods, in this case, the good of self-consciousness.

9. I say "hypothetically" because supporters of abortion rights, especially those who support *Roe v. Wade* or some variant of it, necessarily support restrictions on abortion. *Roe*, it must be remembered, only authorized *unrestricted* abortion in the first trimester, then stated requirements for mid-term and late-term abortions. I do not qualify the previous sentence with "hypothetically" since there are pro-life extremists who do advocate the exact position referred to in the sentence, including Orrin Hatch, U.S. senator from Utah, who denies that any exceptions can be made for abortion, so highly—absolutely, I would say—does he honor fetal life and seek to afford it absolute protection. On the other hand, it must be remembered that pro-choice advocates can assert choice as an absolute value, something that apparently happened in many of the "friend (*amici*) of the Court" briefs that were presented for deliberation in *Roe v. Wade*. Justice Blackmun alludes to this absolutism for choice when he writes in *Roe*, "[S]ome *amici* argue that the woman's right is absolute and that she is entitled to terminate her pregnancy at whatever time, in whatever way, and for whatever reason she alone chooses. With this we do not agree." (Quoted from excerpted decision as found in "Majority Opinion in *Roe v. Wade*," in Sommers and Sommers, *Virtue and Vice in Everyday Life*, 880.

10. See Edmund N. Santurri, *Perplexity in the Moral Life: Philosophical and Theological Considerations* (Charlottesville: University Press of Virginia, 1987), 2, for definition and discussion of actual moral dilemmas.

11. Judith Jarvis Thomson, "A Defense of Abortion," in Joel Fineberg, ed., *The Problem of Abortion*, 2nd ed. (Belmont, CA: Wadsworth, 1973, 1984), 187.

12. *Roe v. Wade*, 410 U.S. 113, 93 S.CT. 705, 35 L.ED.2D. 146 (1973). *Roe v Wade* established a trimester scheme in which abortion is legally permitted without any state interference during the first twelve weeks of pregnancy (i.e., the first trimester). An abortion during the second trimester can only be performed with a doctor's approval; and the state identifies a compelling interest in fetal life during the third trimester, and abortions are thus restricted to those that prove an endangerment to the mother's life. It should be noted that the trimester scheme was challenged by the subsequent *Webster v. Reproductive Health Services* decision in 1989 (492 U.S. 490).

13. Russia is losing population: 1991 statistics indicate that the death rate is higher than the birth rate. Concern has been expressed in official circles, if not so much about the high abortion rate, at least about the low birth rate, and there have been efforts to promote an increase in the birth rate. This is evidence that the good of life ingredient in pregnancy is recognized as a good and that efforts are being made to promote that good.

14. Cultural relativism—the idea that practices vary from cultural setting to cultural setting—is a descriptive fact of life. This identifies the reality of what is sometimes called sociological relativism (e.g., the descriptive fact that Americans eat with forks, the Japanese with chopsticks). Moral relativism, however, holds that there is no standard of valuation that would permit one to evaluate another person or culture's moral practices, which is an incoherent perspective. For a classic rejection of moral relativism, see John Hospers, *Human Conduct* (New York: Harcourt Brace Jovanovich, 1961).

15. Novelist Gore Vidal has played with apocalyptic protagonists who view death—not life—as a good in his novels *Messiah* (New York: Ballantine, 1984) and *Kalki* (New York: Ballantine, 1978). The fact that certain individuals or even cultures do not accept a universal good as good does not mean that the good is purely relative and therefore not universal. Universal is not an absolute term, as if it were descriptively true that each good of life is acknowledged as such absolutely, without exception, and according to unanimous consent. Again, this is not a perfect world, and whether one takes the view that failing to honor a good of life as good is the result of ignorance or a perverse will, the fact that human beings act against goods of life is also an aspect of a fundamental moral ontology of human being. That human beings are capable of wrongdoing, evil, perversity, and defiance of goodness does not mean that the goods of life are not universal. It means, rather, that those who offend against that good are violating the good and deserve moral reproach and censure from the larger moral community.

## CHAPTER 2. THE MORAL PRESUMPTION AT ISSUE IN ABORTION

1. Thomas E. McCollough, *The Moral Imagination and Public Life* (Chatham, NJ: Chatham House, 1991), 19. McCollough offers a good analysis of moral community and the role of the moral imagination in framing those communities. He does not construe moral

community around moral presumptions, and I do not wish to infer that this is a philosophical construct he necessarily affirms.

2. That moral presumptions are unconscious opens us to the possibility of self-deception in the moral life, for it is possible to act contrary to a deeply avowed moral presumption but interpret that action, wrongly, as consistent with the moral presumption. We do this not only because we want or desire something that is contrary to the moral presumption, but because we do not want to violate the moral presumption or understand ourselves as offending it—so deeply do our moral presumptions hold us. For more on this, see Lloyd H. Steffen, *Self-Deception and the Common Life* (New York: Peter Lang, 1986), 233–300.

3. The beliefs in question are technically *dispositional beliefs*; that is, they are beliefs that dispose a person to act a certain way, and on the basis of that action, one can infer and impute the belief that governs the action. Dispositional beliefs reveal themselves in and through our actions, just as one could infer from my opening a door that I intend to pass through the doorway and that I believe that I shall be able to pass through (i.e., it can be inferred that I do not believe I shall be impeded by, say, a brick wall or other obstruction).

Moral presumptions are comprised of dispositional beliefs, which is to say that one can acquire access to the content of persons' moral presumptions by interpreting behavior. We perform our dispositional beliefs in publicly observable ways. By virtue of doing what we do, we reveal the beliefs that dispose us to act one way rather than another. And we can gain access to persons' deeply held, dispositional beliefs by observing their behavior and inferring how their beliefs dispose them to act. From dispositional beliefs we can impute motive and discern intention—we can even discern insincerity, hypocrisy, and self-deception by observing the gap between our most reasonable interpretation of a person's action and the person's own. A moral presumption that values life as good and worthy of being promoted would manifest in publicly observable ways a dispositional belief to that effect. If there is a common moral presumption between persons on the pro-life and pro-choice sides of the abortion issue, we should be able to look at publicly observable behavior and infer from that behavior the beliefs about the value of life that are disposing persons to act consistently with those beliefs.

4. Character is developed through social systems of moral education,

the end of which is the development of persons who are able to embody and promote goodness in their actions and attitudes. We acquire character, which is to say that we develop certain traits and habits, vices and virtues by which we are known in the world. This character, this structure of personality integrity comprised of moral attributes and abilities, reveals itself in behavior, in what we do and how we act. Yet it is not simply action-related, since character expresses who we are—that is, our moral being.

With the acquisition of character, we become constituted as moral persons, and we are encountered as persons who operate in the world from definite and discernible moral presumptions. Others come to know us as reliable and dependable, even morally predictable. People come to know our convictions, what we value, and the extent to which we will seek to promote and defend what we believe to be worthy of our care and protection. We come to be known as persons of character, which is to say, persons who are able to embody our moral presumptions. In knowing our character, others come to know what we believe and value—they come to know us as persons constituted in the light of certain moral presumptions. Gaining access to an individual's moral presumptions is what allows us to encounter the other in his or her being-in-the-world, which is always a being disposed to act in the world in ways that conform to the most deeply seated beliefs and values to which a person is committed.

5. See just abortion criterion 6, Prior-to-Promise, in chapter 5, pp. 106–21.
6. Immanuel Kant, "On a Supposed Right to Tell Lies from Benevolent Motives," in *Kant's Critique of Practical Reason and Other Works*, trans. T. K. Abbott (London: Longmans, Green, 1973). For an engaging Kantian analysis of lying, see Charles Fried, *Right and Wrong* (Cambridge, MA: Harvard University Press, 1978).

## CHAPTER 3. THE FRAMEWORK FOR JUST ABORTION

1. See note 7, Introduction, for some literature on just war theory that might be helpful. The criteria I enunciate here are taken from my article "Applying 'Just War' Standards to the Gulf," 19.
2. Highlighting the precision of technologically advanced weaponry was designed to garner public support for the justness of the war effort, for such weaponry was presented as a way of complying with

the just war demand that non-combatants be protected from direct harm.

3. A well-known article on abortion that seeks to establish criteria for personhood, showing that a fetus does not satisfy them so that aborting a fetus does not constitute a moral violation, led its author to conclude that a neonate also does not satisfy this definition of "person." The logical conclusion of this argument was an endorsement of the possibility of infanticide, which could then be considered morally allowable up to a certain point in a baby's development. See Michael Tooley, "A Defense of Abortion and Infanticide," in Joel Fineberg, ed., *The Problem of Abortion*, 2d ed. (Belmont, CA: Wadsworth, 1973), 120–34. See also Michael Tooley, *Abortion and Infanticide* (Oxford: Clarendon Press, 1983).

4. Richard C. Sparks, *To Treat or Not to Treat: Bioethics and the Handicapped Newborn* (New York, NY: Paulist Press, 1988), 317.

5. Sparks, *To Treat or Not to Treat*, 317.

6. Ibid., 311.

7. Ibid., 316.

8. Ibid., 317.

## CHAPTER 4. THE THEORY OF JUST ABORTION

1. Even religious pro-life persons would want to include criteria other than mere biological vitality, such as some notion of God's concern for the protection of the fetus, or ensoulment, or some other concern that would express a foundation for religious valuation of this particular form of life.

2. Those who take issue with this claim are refusing for some reason to acknowledge the good of life as a *relational* good; and they are thereby mistaking the preeminence of the good of life in a relational matrix or even hierarchy of values for an absolute value.

3. The idea that a woman facing an unwanted pregnancy who decides to bring the fetus to term is no longer confronted with a moral problem strikes me as shortsighted. To bring an unwanted baby into the world and to plan to raise it with the view that it is unwanted is also a moral problem; the prospect of a woman bringing a fetus to term, establishing a nine-month relationship with it, then giving it up for adoption also strikes me as a serious moral problem. Practical evidence of this problem can be found in the fact that many who surrogate for others for money choose not

to proceed with the contract because of the moral connectedness they feel for their baby.

4. The social policy options that would confront a woman in such a situation are distinct from the moral question, for it is certainly possible that a woman may enjoy the political liberty to seek the medical procedure that terminates her pregnancy, whether through surgical abortion or though a medical treatment that has an abortive effect on a fertilized ovum (e.g., RU-486, the abortion pill; or Ovral, the "morning-after" pill). The social policy issue, however, begs the moral question. The moral question is whether aborting a conceptus/fetus can be justified.

5. The argument that "I have a right to do anything I choose with my body" raises the specter of Descartes' ghost in a machine, which I thought philosophical feminism had wanted to do away with. The position reinstates a body-mind dualism by locating in some mysterious center of meaning and value distinct from the body the self-consciousness that claims for itself control over the body and the moral authorization to subject the body to its unchecked power of decision-making. A right to do anything one wants with one's body has the effect of rendering the body an object of instrumental, rather than intrinsic, value; and if it is of instrumental value to me, why should it not be treated instrumentally by others? If something about persons distinct from their bodies is of intrinsic value, the door is opened to justify all those things human beings have done over the centuries to allow harm to come to persons' bodies on the justification that doing so can help to enhance or preserve or even "save" the true center of intrinsic value, whatever it be—the immortal soul, for instance. Such thinking has been used to justify everything from self-flagellation to inquisitorial torture. Holding that the body is of instrumental rather than of intrinsic value to persons endorses rather than subverts domination modes of thinking. If a woman's body is subject to a decision-making authority distinct and separable from the body, the claim that a woman can choose to do anything she wishes with her body expresses a nonrelational view of personal autonomy and an absolutism on the question of choice as objectionable as the absolutism that views fetal life from conception as inviolable.

6. One thinks of China, where the societal need for restraint in population growth in the light of scarce resources has led to a social policy that practically forces a woman to resort to abortion if more than one child is born to a family. Although it would require a

great deal of argumentation to establish a moral justification for the state instituting such a social policy, it is not inconceivable that this could be done under just abortion theory if social circumstances were sufficiently dire. I don't endorse such an argument, but I reiterate that the state is not the appropriate legitimate authority to determine whether a particular pregnancy is wanted or unwanted, even though the state obviously has an interest in broader social policy issues related to population growth (e.g., Russia) and control (e.g., China).

7. Justifying abortion must begin with a recognition that the pregnancy is unwanted. While the particular reasons involved in determining that a pregnancy is unwanted go to issues of just cause (see criterion 2, pp. 83–94), the question at the outset is this: Who decides that a particular pregnancy is unwanted? Many persons involved with the pregnant woman may have views on this question, including the father, the immediate family, and the religious, moral, social, and economic community of which the woman is a part. And these other persons may certainly be forced to think through this issue of pregnancy desirability if, for some medical or psychological reason, the woman is incapacitated and unable to manifest competency and exercise full autonomy. But, those exceptions aside, these others ought not to determine the answer to the desirability question for the woman herself. Were they to do so, the woman, who could easily find herself at odds with these others, might experience moral disenfranchisement and disempowerment. Were she unable to determine the desirability issue, she could rightly claim that she was being disvalued as a person, and that others, who desire the pregnancy such that they are willing to coerce her into bringing the pregnancy to term, were treating her not as an end in herself but as a means to some end that others have established without paying heed to all that she as mother is taking into account as the person most intimately affected and relationally involved in the pregnancy. To avoid coercion, the mother's unique and authoritative position on the question of desirability needs to be acknowledged. A just abortion cannot be envisioned that does not incorporate this concern. The woman herself must be recognized as competent to determine the good of a particular pregnancy in relation to other goods that might be conflicting with that good.

8. Thomson, "A Defense of Abortion," 187.

9. I say "fanatical" because fanatics are persons who hold to positions

with such inflexibility that they would allow themselves to be harmed and destroyed by so doing. A fanatical person would be willing to say, "I accept that a fetus is my moral superior. If my life were threatened by that fetus in some way, I would willingly allow the fetus to come to term and live even if I had to sacrifice my own life to do so." Holding to such a position, which is usually done in the third person (i.e., "She ought to accept that her fetus is her moral superior") rather than the first person, enunciates a position that does not observe prudential reason or even the biblical injunction to love the neighbor as oneself. To allow oneself to be sacrificed to a moral superior, represented by the fetus, is to love the fetus more than oneself and oneself-as-neighbor. So much does this offend against prudential and practical reason, and fundamental commitments to self-regard that are the hallmarks of reasonable and faithful people, that one who held to such an absolutist perspective would be termed not only a moral absolutist but a fanatic as well. See the discussion in chapter 1 about fanaticism.

10. It is worth noting that pro-life persons who are willing to make the exceptions we have discussed so far—abortion to save a mother's life, incest and rape—are actually advocating a restrictive form of pro-choice by these exceptions because they are not holding the fetus to be the mother's moral superior to which she must sacrifice her life if that is required to save the fetus, and because they are not demanding that a woman pregnant by rape or incest get an abortion or not get an abortion—but that she decide what she wants to do. In a definite anti-abortion posture, they are holding open the door to choice—that the pregnant woman choose either to abort or not to abort—and if she does abort, the fact that she became pregnant through rape or incest is sufficient to establish just cause.

11. The ongoing civil war in Bosnia-Herzegovina has shown us once again how rape can be used as an instrument of political-military terrorism. The European Community Commission charged with investigating allegations of atrocities estimated that 20,000 Muslim women had been raped by Serbs as part of the Serbian expansion policy. Rape was used as a deliberate policy instrument, imposing on Muslim women a lasting wound and religious violation that was designed to force the Moslems to internalize the degradation and assault of the war itself. Although many women made pregnant through this policy of terrorism have sought abortions, a controversy arose in February 1993 when Pope John Paul II spoke out opposing abortion for victims of rape in Bosnia-Herzegovina

while also deploring the violence of rape. The Vatican also denied that it had permitted nuns working in danger zones where the threat of assault and rape was high to take birth control pills. The official Roman Catholic teaching on abortion and birth control was thus reiterated during the civil war in Bosnia-Herzegovina, but it provoked outrage in some quarters. The Roman Catholic teaching on abortion would not ascribe to the life created through rape any evil or taint despite the means by which the pregnancy began. Just abortion would not object to that particular point. It would, however, hold that this view as a moral perspective on abortion expresses a moral absolutism that fails to appreciate the full dimension of moral violation experienced by the rape victim. While just abortion would certainly not force a woman who had been raped to abort that fetus, it would object to attempts to restrict access to safe abortion for women who experienced such violation.

12. Medical seriousness also plays a role, since abortion involves tissue loss and the possibility of infection. All things being equal, it is always reasonable to take the least risky course of medical care or treatment, and abortion as a medical procedure is not necessarily the least risky choice when deciding how to deal with an unwanted pregnancy.

13. The medical success criterion is vitally important to the reasoning of *Roe v. Wade*, since the majority decision in *Roe* argues that at the point where proceeding with pregnancy becomes medically safer than abortion (second trimester), the state has a compelling interest in the mother's welfare as well as that of the fetus, so that abortion is now restricted and requires medical justification as a function of protecting the health of the mother and lessening the risk she would face with abortion, which is a risk now deemed to be greater, medically speaking, than that of continued pregnancy.

14. The Soviet rate of abortion was 106 per 1,000 fertile females in 1990, the highest rate in the world. The U.S. was second, with 29 per 1,000. This information is from Yuri Maltsev, "In the Soviet Union—A Medical Nightmare," *Seattle Times*, Aug. 5, 1990, A18. The number of pregnancies statistic is from the article "Abortion in USSR and Other Places," *Chicago Tribune*, July 29, 1990, C3. The article is itself excerpted from Jodi L. Jacobson, *The Global Politics of Abortion* (Washington, D.C.: Worldwatch Institute, 1990). It is worth noting that despite the availability of abortion on demand in the Soviet Union, many women, because of social disapproval and other technological and bureaucratic bar-

riers, have resorted to seeking abortions that are essentially illegal; and so desperate is the state of medical care that reports have surfaced indicating that patients have also resorted to bribes for anesthesia, especially in conjunction with abortion. Czechoslovakia, East Germany, and Hungary kept abortion rates relatively low by encouraging widespread contraceptive use, but in the Soviet Union, there was no sex education in schools, only a compulsory part of the curriculum dealing with marriage laws and the budget of the Soviet family.

## CHAPTER 5. THE THEORY OF JUST ABORTION II

1. Maureen Muldoon, *The Abortion Debate in the United States and Canada: A Source Book* (New York and London: Garland, 1991), 50.
2. Thomas Szasz, "The Ethics of Abortion," *Humanist* 26 (1966): 148.
3. I have not undertaken in this study to recapitulate a history of the Roman Catholic church's position on fetal humanity, although it is not, in my view, a consistent history over the centuries. Understanding that history is very important to understanding how the Roman Catholic church has come to adopt what I consider to be an absolutist view on the question of fetal humanity. (There are also many Protestants who hold to a similar view even if for different reasons, primary among them being the Protestant principle that each individual Christian is responsible for interpreting the Scriptures, so that the Scriptures are interpreted as upholding an absolutist view of fetal humanity—a view that I, as a Protestant, do not share.) For more on the history and diversity of Roman Catholic views on the question of fetal humanity see the article and bibliographic resources offered by Lisa Sowle Cahill, "Abortion," in James F. Childress and John Macquarrie, eds., *The Westminster Dictionary of Christian Ethics*, (Philadelphia: Westminster Press, 1967, 1986), 1–5. See also the helpful collection edited by Patricia Beattie Jung and Thomas A. Shannon, *Abortion and Catholicism: The American Debate* (New York: Crossroad, 1988).
4. I am the father of identical twins; and while I do not know that this happened, my eldest son, who was a single birth, could have been formed by mosaic. Were I to take seriously the metaphysics of the immortal soul as I have offered it here and ascribe a soul to each fertilized egg that developed into one of my sons, it is possible that I could have one son who might have two souls because of mosaic,

while one of my twin sons might have one soul and the other none (or each of them one-half). Holding to a person-from-conception around this ensoulment metaphysics places me in a metaphysically absurd universe; and since my theological view of creation does not yield a metaphysically absurd universe, I find religious views that interpret personhood through a metaphysics of the soul to be unsound and not worthy of my belief.

5. Jane English, "Abortion and the Concept of a Person," reprinted in Mary Vetterling-Braggin, Frederick Elliston, Jane English, eds., *Feminism and Philosophy* (Totowa, NJ: Littlefield, Adams, 1977), 417–28. English writes, "I think it impossible to attain a conclusive answer to the question of whether a fetus is a person" (p. 419). This article makes much of the idea of "resemblance to newborn" that is used so effectively by Peter Wenz in his book on abortion and the Constitution, *Abortion Rights as Religious Freedom* (Philadelphia: Temple University Press, 1992), which I invoke as helpful to thinking through the fetal humanity issue.

6. See the discussion of promise-keeping in chapter 2, pp. 40–41. Just abortion shifts the issue away from fetal humanity per se, which is a philosophical and metaphysical question, and recasts the issue in practical, moral terms. There is no metaphysically certain answer to the question, At what point does the fetus become (or become recognized as) a member of the moral community? There is, however, a practical answer to this question. The fetus, which enjoys the good of life and is already protected by the presumption against abortion, is not ordinarily the object of moral conflict. But given that moral conflict arises over a pregnancy, and a pregnancy is determined to be unwanted, the fetus is entitled to receive protection from the moral community not by virtue of properties it acquires through the process of biological development—for the biological facts of fetal development must still be morally interpreted—but because the mother establishes and enters into a moral relation with the fetus. The point at which the moral conflict over an unwanted pregnancy ought not to be settled by recourse to abortion is when the moral relation between mother and fetus is established. And that moral relation is grounded in the moral practice of promise-keeping.

7. What is of moral interest here is not simply the point in biological development at which the fetus deserves to be considered a member of the moral community. The focus of moral attention is the promise that the mother makes to the child to bring the fetus to

term, for with that promise comes an acknowledgment that the fetus is regarded as if it were a person, a member of the moral community. Promise-keeping is a foundation of the moral life, and to violate promise-keeping is a grave moral offense. To promise to bring the fetus to term is to extend protection to the fetus, which is also to say that aborting a fetus after that promise has been made is a moral offense or violation.

8. Ellis and Beckman, A *Clinical Manual of Gynecology*, 283.

9. *Roe* made a point of justifying first-trimester abortions on grounds that they were less dangerous to the mother than going to term with the pregnancy.

10. Wenz, *Abortion Rights as Religious Freedom*, 178–80.

11. I am aware of arguments and positions like those of Michael Tooley, mentioned earlier, that deny the newborn the status of personhood. My claim, however, is that newborns are admitted into the moral community as a practical matter, which I think is true (that is, it expresses a belief about how the world is and how it actually works). There are persons who argue that developmental insufficiencies present in a newborn could be said to prevent it from being acknowledged as a member of the moral community, which thus exposes the newborn to the possibility of infanticide. My view is that infanticide is morally repugnant, not because people are ignorant that newborns lack the ability to exercise capacities related to personhood, capacities that are not yet realized—what parent does not know that?—but because by the time of birth, moral commitments to the newborn are so strong that as a practical matter, the newborn is regarded as a person in a less controversial way than before birth. This is a descriptive remark about how the moral community—not individual philosophers like Tooley—regards the newborn.

12. One of the complications of holding to the view that the life of a human embryo or a month-old fetus is the moral equivalent of fully endowed members of the moral community (you or me) is that a case could be made that many who hold this view do not, at some deep level, really believe it, at least not to the point where they are prepared to act on that belief. (That is to say that the belief is not dispositional but occurrent—I claim to hold the belief but manifest no behavior expressive of that belief.) I have yet to hear an advocate of the person-from-conception perspective arguing that we should be redirecting our medical research resources to preserve and bring to term those fertilized eggs, estimated at one-half of all

fertilized eggs, that are sloughed off in the early stages of pregnancy, usually because of natural genetic defect. If fertilized eggs
are to be considered persons, then society would be morally obligated to preserve them so that they come to term as is their right—
and increase our percentage of defective newborns by 800 percent,
according to one estimate. The claim that nature (or God) is
performing these abortions hardly seems relevant since the moral
obligation to save a person's life stands regardless of developmental
attributes. Although I refer to biological attributes and I see no way
to avoid involving fetal development, my case is that the moral
meaning of abortion must be tied to those criteria not as if they
were intrinsically obvious demarcation points, but as general
guides that allow us to understand how membership in the moral
community is acquired when certain members of the community
(fetuses, young children, the mentally disabled, even the comatose) lack those characteristics.

13. And they are not functional/operational until sometime around
the twelfth week after birth, which has led Michael Tooley to
defend infanticide and to argue that the newborn itself should not
be entered into the moral community until it is physiologically
capable of being a person. Personhood is a complex notion, and
physiological capability cannot be solely determinative. The fact
that there is a social conferral of personhood status within moral
communities by moral communities is a more critical issue than the
actual possession of what are also arbitrarily determined functional,
instantiated physiological characteristics or attributes.

14. By shifting the focus of the moral issue and the moral offense
involved in a late-term abortion away from the metaphysics of
personhood per se to moral relations and the act of promise-keeping, we take into account the moral reality that something grave
and morally offensive occurs in a late-term abortion. But we also
stop short of condemning the abortion as murder. There are sufficient ambiguities in the fact that personhood is *conferred* in moral
communities, and that the seven-month-old fetus is not yet a
newborn but still only resembles one, to say that the kind of
absolutist condemnation involved in a charge of murder is unwarranted. But a moral offense is still involved, and that offense is that
a promise to nurture and continue life has been broken. Morality
ought not to consider this a trivial offense; as I have said, promise-
keeping, particularly when it pertains to life, is at the foundation
of the moral life, and to offend against that moral institution is to

defy the moral life itself. It defies the need to make and keep one's relational commitments, and it shows a disregard not only for the value of life but also for the good of constancy in character and the good involved in commitment to the value of telling the truth. These are grave moral offenses, as murder is a grave moral offense; but this killing—the killing that takes place in a late-term abortion—is surrounded with sufficient ambiguity, especially with regard to the moral status of the fetus, that calling all such impermissible abortions murder misrepresents the offense.

## CONCLUSION

1. Absolutist perspectives, in a formal sense, must incorporate into the absolute all things, both positive and negative. When moral absolutists act as absolutists and seek to preserve fetal life at all costs, they may endanger the very lives—the fetal lives—they are seeking to protect. This is the fanatical response I discussed earlier, but I would reiterate the contradictory nature of moral absolutism, namely, that it is the nature of a moral absolute to require persons to act to preserve an absolute value by adopting means of protection that are antithetical to the value itself.

2. Paul writes in this verse, "And why not say (as some people slander us by saying that we say), 'Let us do evil that good might come'?—Their condemnation is deserved." The condemnation of the idea do evil that good might result is just: that Christians endorse such a view is, according to this verse, slander.

3. See my "Casting the First Stone: Capital Punishment Is Still a Moral Problem," *Christianity and Crisis* 50, no. 1 (Feb. 5, 1990): 11–16; "The Death Penalty Is Unjust," in Carol Wekesser, ed., *The Death Penalty: Opposing Viewpoints* (San Diego: Greenhaven Press, 1991), 61–66; and "Witness to a Public Death," *Christianity and Crisis* 50, no. 19 (Jan. 7, 1991): 425–27.

4. I suspect that many of those who support the death penalty do so, perhaps unconsciously, by interpreting the convicted criminal as a non-person, as so despicable a being as to be less than human and thus undeserving of possessing life. I deny this—criminals do not lose their fundamental humanity and life by virtue of what they do, and cutting off appeals for justice recognizes the obliteration of humanity that the execution itself performs. That loss of humanity must be assumed in order for an execution to proceed. For an important defense of the view that prisoners on death row are

persons, and not simply in a categorical and philosophical way, see the compelling and agonizing story of Joe Ingle's fifteen-year ministry to death row inmates in Joseph B. Ingle, *Last Rights: Thirteen Fatal Encounters with the State's Justice* (Nashville: Abingdon Press, 1990).

5. Justice Stevens' remarks are taken from *Webster v. Reproductive Health Services*, 492 U.S. 490 (1989), a decision that the state may include findings about life beginning from the moment of conception. For quotation of relevant material and discussion, see Wenz, *Abortion Rights as Religious Freedom*, 81–82, 175–76.

6. Wenz, *Abortion Rights as Religious Freedom*, 82.

7. My denomination, the United Church of Christ, has in General Synod pronouncements on the abortion issue defended and endorsed a woman's right to receive abortion services, thus implying a view of fetal humanity at odds with other religious communities/ organizations/communions who oppose abortion on the basis of holding different views of fetal humanity.

8. I would use a freedom of religion position to argue for a constitutional right to privacy as well. I have a right to believe, under a constitutional guarantee of religious freedom, that there is a God, or that there is no God; that Jesus was divine, or that Jesus was sent by space aliens; that God has ensouled a conceptus, or that there is no soul at all. I am also granted the right not to have to share any of those beliefs with anyone. I can enjoy total privacy with respect to my religious beliefs. My point is that if fetal humanity is a religious belief, then *Roe* could have argued that, which it almost did. Justice Blackmun, the majority opinion author, at one point indicates that so much confusion surrounds the question of fetal humanity (he refers to it, inaccurately, as the question of "when life begins," which I take to be a biological remark about which there is not real dispute) that the judiciary could not possibly claim competence to decide such an issue. But in the next paragraph, Blackmun goes on to explicate the diversity of views surrounding the question of fetal humanity, and his examples are all expressive of religious/metaphysical viewpoints. He refers to the Stoic belief in life at birth, also held by some but not all in the "Jewish faith" and by "a large segment of the Protestant community, insofar as that can be ascertained." One could safely assume the Roman Catholic position on this was well understood by the 1973 Supreme Court, and thus it was also taken into account as a major view. This kind of argument aligns *Roe* for an "establishment

clause," First Amendment protection argument, although the Court did not draw this conclusion but went directly to a defense of privacy, which is certainly an argument that can be made, although it is not an explicit argument, as the Court itself acknowledged. Arguing establishment clause protections would, in my opinion, have prevented constitutional conservatives from making many of the criticisms they subsequently did make, understanding a constitutional conservative to be one who seeks an explicit constitutional guarantee, rather than an implicit one. See Wenz, *Abortion Rights as Religious Freedom*, for a brilliant exposition of the religious question of abortion and the Constitution.

9. We should be reluctant to seek a literal endorsement for or against abortion in the Scriptures, for the Scriptures, because they take the complexity of human history and experience seriously, do not fall on the side of absolutism. Many value absolutists on the abortion issue seek to find in the Scriptures absolute prohibitions against abortion so that they can then invoke divine command to justify their absolutism. I deny that such absolutes are available. My reason for so doing is that one could justify a pro-choice interpretation perhaps with even greater ease. Consider the Passover as a divine defense—not of abortion—but of infanticide, something I have been at pains to evaluate here as not morally controversial but worthy of universal moral condemnation. Yet one could say that Yahweh sent an agent (metaphor for the physician?) to strike down the first-born—which included not only adults but children, even infants, even day-old infants—for a "quality of life" reason, namely, freedom from political oppression. The Passover was instigated to persuade the Pharaoh to release the people of Israel. Could not one respond to pro-life absolutists by arguing that if Yahweh in the Passover willed and caused to come about the death of innocent children—for certainly the day-old first-born of Egypt must have been "innocent"—then God would oppose other kinds of enslavement that an unjust state would impose. If lacking access to abortion could be interpreted as a kind of enslavement or sexual submission to male domination, would not Yahweh also support, in the name of freedom, something so morally serious as the killing of unborn fetuses, which do not possess, in the Hebrew tradition, the moral status of the born? If the Passover is any kind of model of Yahweh's values and the high value freedom takes over the lives of those who impede freedom, this seems a possible point for serious argumentation and biblical interpretation. One could, then,

look to the Passover as an explicit justification for abortion/infanticide for quality of life reasons. I do not defend this point very far except to say that using the Scriptures to justify one's moral position is a tricky game. Although pro-choice persons have not been particularly adept at it, they could learn to cull the Scriptures for stories and verses just as powerful as those verses that pro-life people invoke to support their case with a divine command justification. While I believe as a Christian thinker that the Scriptures address the abortion issue, I do not believe that they explicitly pronounce on the morality of abortion, but rather give guidelines for how such a decision ought to be made faithfully and in keeping with the requirements of love and justice.

# Bibliography

Cahill, Lisa Sowle. "Abortion." In *The Westminster Dictionary of Christian Ethics*, edited by James F. Childress and John Macquarrie. Philadelphia: Westminster Press, 1967, 1986.

Childress, James F. "Just War Theories: The Bases, Interrelations, Priorities and Functions of Their Criteria." *Theological Studies* 39 (September 1978): 427–45.

_____, and John Macquarrie, eds. *The Westminster Dictionary of Christian Ethics.* Philadelphia: Westminster Press, 1967, 1986.

Ellis, Jeffrey W., and Charles R. B. Beckman. *A Clinical Manual of Gynecology.* Norwalk, CT: Appleton-Century-Crofts, 1983.

English, Jane. "Abortion and the Concept of a Person." In *Feminism and Philosophy*, edited by Mary Vetterling-Braggin et al. Totowa, NJ: Littlefield, Adams, 1977.

Fried, Charles. *Right and Wrong.* Cambridge: Harvard University Press, 1978.

Gewirth, Alan. *Human Rights: Essays on Justification and Applications.* Chicago: University of Chicago Press, 1982.

Grisez, Germain, and Russell Shaw. *Beyond the New Morality: The Responsibilities of Freedom.* 2d ed. Notre Dame: University of Notre Dame Press, 1974, 1980.

Hallie, Philip. "From Cruelty to Goodness." In *Vice and Virtue in Everyday Life: Introductory Readings in Ethics*, edited by Christina Hoff Sommers and Fred Sommers. 3d ed. Fort Worth: Harcourt Brace, 1993.

_____. *Lest Innocent Blood Be Shed: The Story of the Village of Le Chambon and How Goodness Happened There.* New York: Harper and Row, 1979.

Hospers, John. *Human Conduct*. New York: Harcourt Brace Jovanovich, 1961.

Ingle, Joseph B. *Last Rights: Thirteen Fatal Encounters with the State's Justice*. Nashville: Abingdon Press, 1990.

Jacobson, Jodi L. *The Global Politics of Abortion*. Washington, DC: Worldwatch Institute, 1990.

Johnson, James Turner. *Can Modern War Be Just?* New Haven: Yale University Press, 1984.

_____. *Just War Traditions and the Restraint of War: A Moral and Historical Inquiry*. Princeton: Princeton University Press, 1981.

Jung, Patricia Beattie, and Thomas A. Shannon. *Abortion and Catholicism: The American Debate*. New York: Crossroad, 1988.

Kant, Immanuel. "On a Supposed Right to Tell Lies from Benevolent Motives." In *Kant's Critique of Practical Reason and Other Works*, translated by T. K. Abbott. London: Longmans, Green, 1973.

Langan, John P. "Elements of St. Augustine's Just War Theory." *Journal of Religious Ethics* 12, no. 1 (1984): 19–38.

McCollough, Thomas E. *The Moral Imagination and Public Life*. Chatham, NJ: Chatham House, 1991.

Muldoon, Maureen. *The Abortion Debate in the United States and Canada: A Source Book*. New York and London: Garland, 1991.

Nicholson, Susan T. "The Roman Catholic Doctrine of Therapeutic Abortion." In *Feminism and Philosophy*, edited by Mary Vetterling-Braggin et al. Totowa, NJ: Littlefield, Adams, 1977.

Noonan, John T., Jr. "Abortion and the Catholic Church: A Summary History." *Natural Law Forum* 12 (1967): 125–31.

Ramsey, Paul. *The Just War: Force and Political Responsibility*. New York: Charles Scribner's Sons, 1968.

Santurri, Edmund N. *Perplexity in the Moral Life: Philosophical and Theological Considerations*. Charlottesville: University Press of Virginia, 1987.

Selzer, Richard. *Mortal Lessons: Notes on the Art of Surgery*. New York: Simon and Schuster, 1974.

Shannon, Thomas A., ed. *War or Peace? The Search for New Answers*. Maryknoll, NY: Orbis Press, 1982.

Sparks, Richard C. *To Treat or Not to Treat: Bioethics and the Handicapped Newborn*. New York: Paulist Press, 1988.

Steffen, Lloyd H. "Abortion and the Conflict of Moral Presumptions." *Papers of the Craigville Theological Colloquy VI: Human Beginnings: Deciding about Life in the Presence of God*. Craigville, MA: Craigville Conference Center, 1989.

_____. "Applying 'Just War' Standards to the Gulf." *Christian Science Monitor*, Feb. 19, 1991, 19.

_____. "Casting the First Stone: Capital Punishment Is Still a Moral Problem." *Christianity and Crisis* 50, no. 1 (Feb. 5, 1990): 11–16.

_____. "The Death Penalty Is Unjust." In *The Death Penalty: Opposing Viewpoints*, edited by Carol Wekesser. San Diego: Greenhaven Press, 1991.

_____. *Self-Deception and the Common Life*. New York: Peter Lang, 1986.

_____. "Witness to a Public Death." *Christianity and Crisis* 50, no. 19 (Jan. 7, 1991): 425–27.

Szasz, Thomas. "The Ethics of Abortion." *Humanist* 26 (1966): 148.

Taylor, Charles. *Sources of the Self: The Making of the Modern Identity*. Cambridge: Harvard University Press, 1989.

Thomson, Judith Jarvis. "A Defense of Abortion." In *The Problem of Abortion*, edited by Joel Fineberg. 2d ed. Belmont, CA: Wadsworth, 1973, 1984.

Tooley, Michael. *Abortion and Infanticide*. Oxford: Clarendon Press, 1983.

_____. "A Defense of Abortion and Infanticide." In *The Problem of Abortion*, edited by Joel Fineberg. 2d ed. Belmont, CA: Wadsworth, 1973, 1984.

Tribe, Laurence H. *Abortion: The Clash of Absolutes*. New York: W. W. Norton, 1990.

Vetterling-Braggin, Mary, Frederick A. Elliston, and Jane English, eds. *Feminism and Philosophy*. Totowa, NJ: Littlefield, Adams, 1977.

Vidal, Gore. *Kalki*. New York: Ballantine, 1978.

_____. *Messiah*. New York: Ballantine, 1984.

Wenz, Peter. *Abortion Rights as Religious Freedom*. Philadelphia: Temple University Press, 1992.

# Index